PRAISE FOR

What We Knew in the Night

"Raven Grimassi shares the heart, soul, and wisdom of the Old Craft elders with his readers, drawing from things half-forgotten and never written, inviting us to know what they knew and incorporate it into our own Craft. This book is a treasure for future generations."

—Christopher Penczak, award-winning author and cofounder of the Temple of Witchcraft

"In *What We Knew in the Night*, Raven Grimassi's last and greatest work, he has given future generations not merely a historical view of witchcraft or a guidebook, but a well-crafted blending of the two, featuring his singular voice. This rendering of Old Witchery offers historical influences and empowering rituals for new and seasoned practitioners alike."

—Amy Blackthorn, author of *Blackthorn's Botanical Magic* and *Sacred Smoke*

"In *What We Knew in the Night,* Raven Grimassi has once again given us a treatise that guides us through a system of witchcraft with passion, clarity, and depth of thought. Raven shares with us his wealth of information that is both old and new in the same instance. With a brief introduction, he launches headfirst into his system that is sure to produce results—provided there is dedication and passion for the Work. If you read only the first chapter, an echo of the entire book itself, you will walk away with much to reflect upon and to practice. Raven advises early on that *What We Knew in the Night* is not a book to be read once; it is to be read, digested, read again, and experienced. In subsequent chapters he treats us to yet more ritual and philosophy, peppered with a good amount of esoteric history. This is a book that deserves to be read in a comfy armchair, while sipping strong tea, loving our Craft, and remembering . . ."

—Andrew Theitic, publisher of *The Witches' Almanac*

"As the final book written by Raven Grimassi before his passing, *What We Knew in the Night: Reawakening the Heart of Witchcraft* is the crown jewel of the legacy of countless contributions that this extraordinary man has provided the witchcraft world. Grimassi provides the deep wisdom that comes from being involved in the witchcraft world for half a century: training, teaching, lecturing, writing books, and interacting with witches and occultists of all types. The book provides what no other book on witchcraft does—a perspective that can only come from both observation and involvement within witchcraft for over sixty years. In the book, Raven reminisces on mysteries that he feels have been lost from those early years before the modern witchcraft and magick renaissance and this book's goal is to preserve that knowledge. These mysteries are those that the witches, regardless of tradition, all knew when gathering together in secret in the night during those early years, hence the title. As such, the insight and sagacity provided within the pages of this book are unparalleled and invaluable to any earnest witch seeking to dive deeper into the heart of the spirit of witchcraft."

—Mat Auryn, author of *Psychic Witch: A Metaphysical Guide to Meditation, Magick, and Manifestation*

"With this extraordinary book, Raven Grimassi has reached across the veil to present us with one last gift: his wealth of knowledge of the Craft, laid out in perfect detail. Filled with the teachings and rites of the Old Ways, and laced with personal anecdotes, *What We Knew in the Night* truly is his legacy: a treasure trove of information that readers will not find elsewhere and a must-read for both seasoned practitioners and those new to the Craft."

—Dorothy Morrison, author of *The Craft* and *Utterly Wicked*

"Sometimes we need to go back before we can meaningfully go forward. In his final work, *What We Knew in the Night*, Raven Grimassi shows us the importance of knowing our past as a collective of magical folk, and he teaches us how we might connect and preserve what was time-honored to the present and to the future. Grimassi's work is a treasure trove of knowledge and practice that he has won not only by study and synthesis, but through his decades of personal practice in the Craft. His teachings, timeworn, tried and true, are a gift to us, and reading this volume is like sitting down with any of the Craft's greatest teachers—Gardner, Valiente, Sanders, the Farrars—and learning straight from them. Grimassi has blessed us with a lasting set of glorious magical instructions, both foundational and beyond. We would do well to heed them."

—Timothy Roderick, author of
Wicca: A Year and A Day, Dark Moon Mysteries, and other books

"*What We Knew in the Night*—such an evocative title, so much information, including some that was almost certainly secret initiatory lore. I found this book to be strangely moving; Raven Grimassi reminds us how different the early witchcraft revival of the mid-20th century was to the widespread popular practices today. He takes us back to primal ancient roots that inspired a new radical movement in the 1960s . . . I was part of that revival in Britain. The core of this book is potent original witch-magic. It reveals the ageless whisper of Ancient Spirit Voices speaking through, and in harmony with, a committed and experienced witch."

—R J Stewart, author of
The UnderWorld Initiation and
many other books on the magical arts

"In *What We Knew in the Night*, Raven Grimassi reintroduces teachings from the '60s and '70s—tending the roots and branches of the modern Western practice of witchcraft and reminding us of who we were by revealing how we've changed. The growth and development of modern practice are solely dependent upon a proper understanding of the past and, in this final treatise, Raven does that in a time-honored, winding-way manner that is sure to guide and inspire both longtime admirers of his work and new practitioners alike. Hail the traveler!"

—Christopher Orapello,
coauthor of *Besom, Stang & Sword*

"Over his long creative career, readers were privileged to walk with Raven Grimassi as his spirituality grew and changed. His last books reveal a man who walked his talk, one who wore his beliefs on his sleeve, as well as his sense of humor. This final book—*What We Knew in the Night: Reawakening the Heart of Witchcraft*—does not disappoint. It is rich and generous and beautiful. It is Grimassi at his best."

—H. Byron Ballard, author of
Earth Works: Ceremonies in Tower Time

what we knew in the night

REAWAKENING THE HEART OF WITCHCRAFT

Raven Grimassi

WEISER BOOKS

This edition first published in 2019 by Weiser Books, an imprint of
Red Wheel/Weiser, LLC
With offices at:
65 Parker Street, Suite 7
Newburyport, MA 01950
www.redwheelweiser.com

ISBN: 978-1-57863-651-8
Library of Congress Cataloging-in-Publication Data available upon request.

Cover design by Kathryn Sky-Peck
Illustrations by Deidra Catero
Interior by Steve Amarillo / Urban Design LLC
Typeset in Sabon, Athelas, Futura, Myriad Pro, and Colby Compressed

Printed in the United States of America
LB
10 9 8 7 6 5 4 3 2 1

DEDICATION

To those who before us preserved and passed on the Ways.

To the current living light-bearers who tend the Sacred Flame.

To the future generation into whose hands pass what is ever ancient and ever new.

We are all sorcerers and,
live in a wonderland of marvel
and beauty if we did but know it.

—CHARLES GODFREY LELAND, *GYPSY SORCERY AND FORTUNE-TELLING*

CONTENTS

PREFACE

The material in this book does not represent an ancient tradition that survived countless centuries. Instead, it presents a spiritual legacy—or perhaps more accurately, it rises from a mystical lineage. The core concepts are timeless.

I have assembled much of what I was taught over the past decades along with things I personally developed as well. It is, in effect, a compilation of my experiences and beliefs over almost fifty years of adult practice in the Arts of Witchery.

The overall system detailed in the following pages did not exist as a whole prior to me writing it. Only the teachings on the quintessence and related material have a single earlier origin. The rest of the material is drawn from a variety of sources and teachers over several decades. Some of this is old and some is relatively modern. The commonality between it all is the rootedness; it is what I call Old Witchery, as opposed to contemporary forms.

In the case of the Witch's ring, the cauldron, and the athame, I have added some new teachings and instructions. In other words, this added material is not originally part of the older Craft. These newer elements will be easy to spot and need no further discussion. I include them for relevance to a new generation.

My goal in this book is to share key and foundational elements that I believe are worth preserving. Many of them are lost to a new generation, but they are important parts of our history and our lineage as Witches.

There was and is a process that delivers the deep ways of the Witch's Arts. This process contains the pieces that together form the Witch's knowledge, and this knowledge moves the Witch to realizations that come only from personal experience.

In these pages, I have placed many of the vital pieces. They are not all put into a linear order, meaning not always in one single chapter in a step-by-step fashion. The true seeker must reflect upon themes delivered in earlier chapters to capture and complete that which fills in the in-between spaces.

Enlightenment does not lie as much in the words being spoken as it does in the context of what is being revealed. Each chapter brings context to what is being unveiled throughout the book. It is the hunter-gatherer approach versus the spoon-fed method of teaching. To fully understand this book, it needs to be read at least twice. If it's results you seek, then I encourage you in this effort.

As you read on, bear in mind that I am using an old Pagan model with roots in pre-Christian European beliefs and practices. I include the key elements that convey the mystical world as our ancestors knew it in their time. Most noted is the Antlered God, remnants of whom are found in folk celebrations throughout Europe. I use this to tie in the elements of Witchcraft as we knew them in the 1960s and as they eventually evolved into the ways of modern Witchcraft.

INTRODUCTION

It was through various writings in the 1950s and 1960s that the topic of modern Witchcraft entered into mainstream society. Individuals such as Gerald Gardner, Alex Sanders, Sybil Leek, and Doreen Valiente rose to celebrity status.

Earlier, in the late 1800s, a man named Charles Godfrey Leland wrote about Italian Witchcraft. His writings were very influential on what later became Wicca. Leland was the first to write about living people who openly claimed to be Witches and who admittedly practiced Witchcraft. He referred to this as the Old Religion (of Italy).

Throughout my book, we will explore Witchcraft and its ways as they existed in the 1960s, before so many changes would later take place. We will journey from there to the contemporary state of modern Witchcraft and Wicca. Much has been altered and changed over the decades, and some things have been lost or jettisoned along the way. Other things were simply unknown to various authors whose backgrounds did not include having been passed the old teachings. So, they taught a philosophy of "Do whatever feels right."

Many popular writers of the 1980s and onward promoted the idea of a self-styled form of Witchcraft with an emphasis on self-initiation and personal intuition. In doing so, they bypassed the time-proven and time-honored traditional ways of Witchcraft that came before them. As a result, readers who "cut their teeth" on books from the 1980s onward were typically not exposed to the older foundations, the older Rooted Ways. That is, of course, a general statement, and there are many exceptions.

My early experiences in Witchcraft came from my childhood through what I call a "peasant tradition" of Witchcraft rooted in Old Europe. Later, in the summer of 1969, I first encountered the greater Witchcraft/Wiccan community at large. It began with a chance meeting at a shop in Old Town, San Diego, called Pooh's Pantry. It was primarily an herbal tea shop but featured a wide variety of dried herbs as well. In the 1960s, "witch shops" were few and far between, if they existed at all, which meant that we found our supplies in other ways. At the time the closest metaphysical shop to me was in San Francisco—a nine-hour drive. From time to time, I made the trip to acquire things that I could not obtain elsewhere. This significant effort made the items I obtained there very important and meaningful to me, and therefore they felt quite powerful as well. There is an old teaching in this, if you care to take note.

My first trip to Pooh's Pantry caught the attention of a young woman named Elizabeth who managed the shop and worked at the checkout counter. She commented on the collection of herbs I set on the counter, saying that they would not make very good tea. She then quickly added that they were "good for other things" and gave me a knowing smile. I was intrigued, to say the least.

This chance meeting eventually ushered me into the Witchcraft/Wiccan community in the San Diego area. Elizabeth directed me to a man named Don, who managed a bookstore called Oracle Books. He, in turn, introduced me to Miranda, who went by the name Lady Heather. She ran a coven in San Diego and through her I was eventually initiated and became one of its members.

I spent most of the 1960s and '70s living in San Diego, California. The city hosts a large U.S. Navy port, which brings in naval personnel from all over the country and those serving in various parts of the world. What I found most striking was meeting these people and discovering our commonality when it came to the ways of Witchcraft. Back in those days, when you met people calling themselves Witches or Wiccans, you knew their tenets of belief. You also knew their pantheon and their terminology. We were all on the same page. Today, this is no longer the case, as so much has changed over the decades.

During the 1960s and '70s, learning about Witchcraft in a larger sense was a matter of being introduced to others, or being brought into some form of contact with others. Most memorable are the times I was driven by friends to meet a long-practicing Witch here and there. Looking back today, I don't think the majority of these people were actually Witches in the commonly understood sense. However, I firmly believe that some of them were—particularly those who moved here from places like Romania, Hungary, Poland, Germany, and Italy. What they independently taught was too similar to one another to have been a coincidence.

Meeting people serving in the Navy was confirming of the larger picture in terms of Witchcraft and Wicca. In most cases they did not know each other, and yet having come from all over the world they knew the same things; they practiced the same Craft. This gave me confidence in the foundations and cohesiveness of Witchcraft/Wicca as a whole. I believed that we shared something that preexisted us all.

In that light, one of the goals of this book is to pass on the things we once passed on to one another back in those days. As Witches, this was what we knew in the night. We were taught the ways as we stood in candlelit circles, knelt in the forest beneath the full moon, and meditated in the "astral temple" of one tradition or another. There were also the voices of spirit-teachers who spoke to us in various ways. In the final analysis, all of this opened the way to gaining a personal gnosis when we bathed in the light of the full moon, heard the voice of the wind, and communed with the same spirits who once taught our ancestors.

In the chapters ahead, you will find many of the foundations and reasons behind what we do in modern Witchcraft. Additionally, you will be shown the keys that unlock the mysteries within the beliefs and practices of modern Witchcraft. To that end, chapters 1 and 5 will provide you with a great deal of connective and inner information. In chapters 7 and 8 you will discover the underlying mystical elements of Witchcraft as a system. Additionally, you will be provided with the spirit-mindedness or "religious" elements that comprise the ways and beliefs of our pre-Christian European ancestors. The rest of the book is built upon these foundations and will provide you with methods to apply these key elements.

NOTICE TO THE READER

Please do not skim this book. There are many important things you will miss by skipping around in the chapters. I have intentionally placed key teachings here and there throughout the chapters in the order that you need to encounter them.

If you skim this book, you will lose context, which is all important to understanding.

If you skip around, you will likely not even find some of the important teachings.

Also, if you have missed the preface and introduction, please go back and read them, as they will help you to better understand the material and what it has to offer.

CHAPTER ONE

WHAT WE KNEW IN THE NIGHT

As to the past, it is because of what is there, that I look back: not because I do not see what is here today, or may be here tomorrow. It is because of what is to be gained that I look back: of what is supremely worth knowing there, of knowing intimately: of what is supremely worth remembering . . .

—William Sharp, *A Memoir*

As mentioned in the introduction, I first encountered the Witchcraft/Wiccan community in the summer of 1969. I think back upon what I learned of Witchcraft in those days of my youth, and my memory is carried upon a mystical scent that reminds me of that distant time: damp moss, and rich earth; night-blooming jasmine, wisteria, and primal forest.

Witchcraft is, among other things, a sentient spirit. It comes to you, if it recognizes and acknowledges you. It resides within you and passes out through you into the world. You, as a Witch, are the in-between place, which is the most magical of all places.

In this chapter I will pass to you many of the things that were passed to me so long ago it seems now. I've had teachers who were human and others who were not. However, one doesn't learn to be a Witch; you either are one or you are not. What we can and do learn is the Arts of Witchcraft; we learn the ways of the Witch. Knowing you are a Witch is a matter of inner discovery. It's recognition and it's acknowledgment. You would not have been drawn to this book if there weren't something of the Witch already inside you.

The word *recognize* means "to know again," and this is an important element. Many people have been Witches in past lives. The word *acknowledge* means "to accept or admit the existence or truth of something." This is the inner knowing, the personal gnosis, and it needs no outside validation. Being a Witch is in your blood, even though it may not be in your lineage. Its essence is a beacon, and as a result there are forces that will be drawn to you (and you to them).

Witchcraft has long been associated with the night and with the moon. We can safely say that it is primarily a lunar path. In ancient pre-Christian writings, we find a goddess of Witchcraft but no specific mention of a god of Witchcraft. The god arrives much later in the writings, and his roots are woodland in nature. He is antlered, and then later he is horned. He is a stag, and then a goat, and eventually a bull. The latter arises in the Christian era when we find the image of the devil, who most often sports a pair of bull horns. Later still, in the Victorian era, is a return to goat horn imagery. Here again horns are sported by the devil in the popular art of the period. In any form, the old god remains in the bone memory of the earth.

In those contemporary forms of Witchcraft and Wicca that include a god, he is most often viewed as a solar deity. In his modern mythos, we see a mated pair, the goddess of the moon and the god of the sun. However, in the 1960s, the god was viewed more as an agricultural figure than the direct god of the sun per se. It was inevitable that the Lord of Plants (also known as the Harvest Lord) would eventually become strongly connected with the sun's role in plant life. Over the following decades, the god took on a greater role as the personification of the sun god. With the ongoing development of the wheel of the year theme, his celestial nature dominated his woodland and agricultural foundations. He became the newborn light at the winter solstice. Today, the evergreen decorations of the season seem like a vestige memory of his early forest nature. We'll talk of him more in forthcoming chapters, but for now let's return to the goddess and to the night.

It is popular today to think of Witchcraft as a practice instead of a religion or a spiritual path. In the 1960s, we thought of it as the old religion of Europe. Ancient pre-Christian writings depict the Witch Medea as a priestess of the goddess Hecate. In the tales written of her, Medea performs rituals in a circle traced upon the ground, and within the circle is an altar at which she calls upon Hecate. The seemingly religious undertones of that did not escape us back in the day.

The 1960s was a time of breaking away from social norms; this included religion. Many young people struggled with the concept of god dwelling in heaven and judging the lives of humans by a set of ten laws reportedly given to Moses: if you obeyed the laws, then you entered into Paradise; but if you failed to do so, then you were sent into eternal torment. We found that to be an odd position for divinity to take in general. As a result, a large number of people turned to mysticism, foreign spiritual pursuits, and Witchcraft/Wicca.

In those days, Witchcraft and Wicca were one and the same; we made no distinction between the two. Today, the two seem to be whatever anyone wants them to be at any given time of day or night. While we may have gained some freedom in this view, unfortunately we have equally distanced ourselves from the roots of our origin. This complicates the matter.

The primary goal of this book is to reintroduce the Rooted Ways of Witchcraft. I see this in the same way as rebooting one's computer when something seems to be causing conflicts or hindering the smooth operation of the system. The material in this book is foundational; it is the core of Witchery. Perhaps you wondered about the title, "What We Knew in the Night," and thought it should be "What We *Know* in the Night." The title I chose indicates something almost forgotten (or of a former state of things). It is intentional because there are things absent in contemporary Witchcraft when compared with earlier times. In the 1980s, the writings on Witchcraft shifted from traditional ways to intuitive ways. The emphasis focused upon doing whatever feels right and customizing things as one goes along. There were both gains and losses in this new approach.

Over the years, I have come to envision the Craft as an old tree. It has it roots, which are the oldest part. The roots provide nourishment for the tree and keep the tree in place so that it does not topple over. The tree also has a trunk, and this is the established presence for all to see its place in the world. Additionally, the tree puts forth new branches and flowers/fruits in each new season. I liken this to the new practitioners and the new systems of Witchcraft that arise over the years. However, if no one (or no thing) tends the roots, if we offer nothing to sustain the tree, it eventually withers and dies. The roots go unseen, but what is unseen truly matters in the ways of Witchcraft.

For the purposes of this book, I will refer to its material and teachings as the Rooted Ways. What I offer here is a system that I have assembled from pieces passed on to me as well as those I've stumbled upon over the decades. I will also include some things I developed on my own. Please note that I am not presenting the material in this book as a surviving tradition or even a preexisting tradition into which I was initiated. It is not; instead, it is an assembled system from the oldest ways of which I have personal knowledge and experience. It is *e pluribus unum*—the one comprised of many parts.

THE TEACHINGS ON NIGHT

The old teachings of Night arise from what can be called the spirit-mindedness of our forest-dwelling ancestors. Daylight was a time of dealing with survival needs, gathering eatables and hunting animals to sustain the tribe. Night was a time for withdrawing into the tree branches beneath the stars and moon for protection against predators. More importantly, it was a time for contemplation, a time for listening, and a time to slip off into the realms of dreams. It was in the blackness of night that our ancestors formulated the enchanted world comprised of spirits and entities.

The stewards of the night are the stars and the moon. They pass the secret mystical essence into the branches of the trees, which hold this for the Witch to pick the forbidden fruit. The stars look down with countless eyes and watch from on high. The moon sheds its light upon the forest branches, and the wind moves the Witch in the night breeze, calling and beckoning her or him.

The night is conscious and self-aware. It is the time of the Witch. In ancient Greek mythology, night is personified as a goddess. Nox (or Nix) is one of the most common names for night as a deity. She is born of Chaos and she later gives birth to Hypnos (sleep), Death, the Fates, and the Oneiroi (dreams). These are the magical offspring of Night, as well as connections to various long-held beliefs and practices associated with Witchcraft.

In the Rooted Ways, night is the *origin*. It is the setting that the Witch enters into for magic and ritual. Night is the blackness of procreation, for everything issues forth from blackness into light. We ourselves were born from the blackness of the womb into the world of light.

My use of "blackness" versus "darkness" here is intentional. It is commonplace to say that the night is dark, meaning the absence of the sun's light. However, to the Witch of the Rooted Ways, the sun is not the defining factor of all things. Night is not the absence of the sun; it is its own realm and its own manifestation. No one defines daylight as the absence of the dark night. Why limit the definition of night to the absence of the bright sun? Certainly, before any suns were created in the universe, there was the blackness of outer space. I cannot say "the *darkness* of outer space" because no light preexisted to be able to speak of darkness as the absence of light. There was only blackness, and it was first.

As a Witch of the Rooted Ways, I regard darkness as a refusal of light. In this view, darkness is a mentality. It is conducive to evil. There are people with dark hearts and there are dark spirits and entities. They reject light and remain separated from its blessings. It is a choice. Blackness is not a choice; it is the sacred night, just as sunlight reveals the blessed day. Two realms are connected and yet independent.

The birth or the awakening of the Witch takes place in the night. In the blackness, the Witch arises and meets the illumination of the full moon. However, the first immersion is into the essence of the power of night. In the Rooted Ways we call this the "black mist" or the "mystical waft of the night." (This process will be explained more in the next chapter.)

Because Night is viewed as both origin and birther, the color black is significant. In the Rooted Ways, Witches wear black hooded robes. One of the stories passed around in the '60s told us that Witches wore black at their night gatherings in order to be able to seemingly disappear if danger approached. This was accomplished by covering the head and face with the hood and pulling the hands deep inside the sleeves of the robe. In the night, with the skin completely covered within the black robe, and all fires extinguished, the Witch was seemingly rendered invisible.

The power of night is its inherent procreative nature. However, night also receives into itself all things that perish in the material world. Out of blackness all things emerge into the world of light (as previously mentioned, you and I emerged from the blackness of the womb). This principle is symbolized by the black cauldron, which often appears in imagery with a skull set in front of it. In addition, a set of crossbones is sometimes placed with the skull. The skull represents the spirits of the dead and the "bone memory" that resides in it after death. The crossbones symbolize walking the Path of the Witch in the night. In this we are the kindred of the night.

Night, and the theme of Witchcraft, leads us to the ancient goddess known as Hecate, whose festival day in ancient Greece was celebrated on the last day of November. One ancient writer mentions a small altar set to Hecate during the festival of Diana (August 13–15). For some people this has confused the date of Hecate's festival, conflating it with Diana's festival date. But in ancient Greco-Roman times, it was typical to begin rituals and magical work by first evoking Hecate. Therefore, the presence of an altar to Hecate at the celebration of another goddess is not surprising.

The first recorded mention of Hecate is found in the ancient Greek writings of Hesiod, who refers to her as a Titan who fought on the side of the Olympian gods. Hesiod portrays Hecate as a goddess who grants victory, success, and abundance. It is not until the fourth century BCE that Hecate is identified with Witchcraft. She then becomes the Mistress of Witchcraft. It is around this same time that Hecate is associated with the Underworld.

As previously mentioned, ancient writers tell us that Hecate is the first deity to call before doing any magical work or performing a ritual. She, in essence, opens the portals that stand between the human world and the spirit world. This lets the magic in and the magic out, so to speak.

Ancient Roman writers, such as Horace, regard Hecate as a triple goddess comprised of Hecate, Diana, and Proserpina. One example is found in the tale of Medea, where she speaks an evocation:

Diana, who commands silence when secret mysteries are performed, I invoke you.

Hecate of the three faces, who knows all my designs, and comes to help the incantations and the craft of the witches, I invoke you. . . .

Proserpina, night-wandering queen, I invoke you.

Hecate, Diana, Proserpina, look kindly now upon this undertaking.[1]

In this text we find the reference to night as the faithful keeper of Witches' secrets. The things Witches came to know in the night were concealed from others by the starry black veil that covered the world from above.

Associated with night is a race of beings known as the Watchers. In the earliest lore, they are said to be the stars (the eyes of night that are ever watchful). In Hebrew writings, we also find a type of angel called a Watcher. This comes from the noncanonical biblical Book of Enoch. In the 1960s we did not readily include concepts from non-European cultures. If memory serves me well, the Hebrew material was added sometime in the 1970s. This same time period drew in the concepts of chakras, mudras, karma, and the Akashic records. This began to obscure the old European roots and foundations. What we knew in the night beneath the full moon started to be dispersed by a different light arriving from Eastern culture.

---

1 Raven Grimassi, "The Roots of Italian Witchcraft," Stregheria, *www.stregheria.com.*

The oldest idea of the Watchers is rooted in star veneration. There is a fate-related connection here that is tied to astrology, and therefore one's fate can be thought of as something influenced by the Watchers. In chapter 5 on Old Magic this idea is further explored. For now, let us stay with the concept of the Watchers as star-beings.

In my book *Wiccan Mysteries*, I wrote about the Watchers being linked to specific stars. In the early stellar cults these stars were called "lords," and they marked the common cardinal points in astrology:

- Aldebaran, marking the vernal equinox, held the position Watcher of the East.
- Regulus, marking the summer solstice, held the position Watcher of the South.
- Antares, marking the autumn equinox, held the position Watcher of the West.
- Fomalhaut, marking the winter solstice, held the position Watcher of the North.

In the 1960s, references to the Watchers included such titles as "Dread Lords of the Outer Spaces" and "Old Ones of the Starry Dome," among others. In addition to recording the actions of the Witch, the Watchers were said to be the escorts of the dead, ushering them into another realm. The earliest idea was that souls went to reside in the lunar realm, where they awaited rebirth. This theme is tied to ancient Greek philosophers who connected the gathering of souls to the increasing light of the moon.

The moon was said to travel across the night gathering up the recently dead. The dead were then contained by the moon when it set in the Underworld. As the moon rose each night, it glowed with the light of the collected souls until it was eventually full, a full moon. Afterward, on each subsequent night, the moon gradually released the souls back into life on earth (reincarnation) or to another realm in which the soul required a different experience. As souls were set free, the light of the moon decreased. This was reflected in the waning light of the moon.

Another idea about where the dead traveled to was called the Summerland (a concept some people say was borrowed from nineteenth-century theologians and spirit mediums). Here the dead rested in an earth-like place that was always in the season of summer. In an associated mythos, the Summerland was filled with all the creatures and beings of ancient myth and legend. It was a pleasant and comforting view of the afterlife for many decades within modern Witchcraft. Sometime in the '80s or '90s, the idea of the death experience took on the concept of a "rainbow bridge" leading to a less defined afterlife experience. In its evolution the afterlife came to be about a place where pets and their former owners reunited.

In the Rooted Ways, teachings about the dead and the afterlife were tied to ancient lore about trees and reincarnation. In old European lore, the dead await rebirth inside a tree and are reborn through hollows in the trunk. Trees were also thought of as bridging the worlds. In this concept, they join together the three great realms of ancient belief: above, below, and in-between.

In his poem *The Theogony*, the ancient Greek writer Hesiod points to Hecate as the goddess of these three great realms. He says she was a Titan who fought on the side of the Olympians in an ancient war of the gods. Zeus rewarded Hecate by allowing her to keep her former status, meaning that she was already the Great Goddess of the Three Known Realms. The tree connection is clear when we note the ancient time-honored custom of erecting tree trunks at a crossroads to honor her.

In time, Hecate became associated with the dead and with the doorway into the Underworld. The dead also became associated with crossroads, where they were said to gather. Once gathered, Hecate would lead them into the realm of the dead. In still later lore, the dead became part of her midnight train that follows her as she flies across the night sky.

The idea of Hecate, the Night, and the Dead connects us with the theme of the Otherworld or spirit realm. It is here that we find the mystical moon tree. The moon tree was a feature of Witchcraft in the 1960s, but by the '80s it had slipped away into obscurity. To better understand this tree, we must look to the roots of the lore from which it arose. We find this in the Inner Mystery teachings.

Tree branches viewed against the backdrop of the moon look very much like bridges or pathways leading up to the moon.

One model for the tree in the Inner Mysteries can be found in the system I practice, which is known as the Ash, Birch and Willow system of Old Witchery. This system is one of the few authentic Mystery Traditions of Witchcraft still operating in the world today. In it, we find the essential moon tree under the name of the Tree of Luneya. Luneya is envisioned as a lunar realm in which souls await rebirth. In its imagery, the tree is white with branches reaching up to seemingly touch the full moon.

In the associated mythos, souls of the dead travel up along the branches to reach the lunar realm. In Luneya, the souls rest, reflect, and prepare for rebirth. The return to physical life in the mortal realm begins with souls journeying back down the branch pathways. They then emerge from the white tree back into material life again.

In a meditation I had with the forest, I asked it, "What happens when I die?" The forest instantly replied, "It is simple. When you die, I will breathe you in, hold you for a moment, and then breathe you back into life." For me, this experience solidified the teachings of the tree. We are part of the cycle of life upon the earth; we are not separate from it as human beings. What happens to all things here also happens to us. The cycle of nature is birth, life, death, and renewal.

Returning to the idea of the old moon tree, it is a mystical design that encapsulates the metaphysical concepts pertaining to it. The basic design shows a trellis enclosing a pole with interlacing slats. These represent how all things are intertwined. Hung along the outside arch of the trellis are lighted lamps representing all the full moons in a year. In the center is a wooden pole, known as a *hekataia* or *hekataeon*. This is symbolic of the classic tree pole set at the crossroads in ancient times.

The image of the full moon flanked by lunar crescents is a sign of what lies beyond entrance. The large white orb that rests on top of the trellis also symbolizes the sacred fruit of the moon, which bestows enlightenment. In the associated lore, the moon tree only bears a single round white fruit once each month. This is, of course, the moon itself as a mystical concept. To reach up, pluck the fruit, and take it down was to draw the moon to oneself.

The image of the moon tree is, in effect, a portal to the lunar realm.

The night teachings connected to the moon tree bring us the figure of the mystical serpent. In the tale, the Witch discovers the single white fruit that hangs from an inner branch. This is the fruit of enlightenment that must be tasted exactly where it is picked. It cannot be brought out and given to another person. However, what it bestows, the Witch can in turn bring to others in the form of its teachings. Ultimately, the teachings allow the student to find his or her own encounter with the moon tree and to taste its fruit directly.

In the lore of the moon tree, we find the serpent wrapped around the white fruit of enlightenment. To obtain the fruit, the Witch must risk the bite of the serpent (just as one must risk the rose thorn to obtain the blossom). These are the Blood Mysteries, and they join with the cycle of the moon and menstrual blood. The cycle of life is reflected in the cycles of the moon. The flow of women's blood is tied to the portal of the moon tree. In its inner symbolism, the moon tree represents female genitalia. Here the vagina is the gate, and behind the gate is the womb, which is the black cauldron of the Underworld. The bite of the snake is obvious enough.

In the Witchcraft of the 1960s there were teachings about a woman's body being the natural altar. The basic idea was more popular as a concept than it was as an actual practice. However, in such a practice, a nude woman would lie on her back with her heels pressed back against her buttocks. A witching cup rested on her navel, which she held in place with both hands. Her bent legs represented the twin pillars of the temple, and her vagina was the entryway. Ritual and magical items were sanctified by anointing them at the portal. I remember one woman who became angry about this teaching, and she confronted the teacher, who responded, "If you don't think your vagina is sacred, then you should be mad at yourself—not mad at me!" It was a most unpleasant moment for all of us attending the class.

Let's return to the serpent in the moon tree—the Initiator and Guardian of the Threshold. In ancient times snakes were placed inside grain storages to keep rodents from eating all the supplies. In this light, the serpent was a guardian and protector of the seed. This ties the serpent to the cycle of the grain, and therefore to the Grain

Mysteries of Old Europe. Here we see the seed as the hidden creator, the generator of life. In this light it is the initiator, which (by association) ties the serpent to the role as well.

In the serpent lore, the fangs of the serpent penetrate those who touch the fruit. Add to this the phallic appearance of the serpent, and things begin to entwine in the mystical sense.

To be penetrated by the serpent, and to receive its essence, is the intoxication of the Witch in the night. This mystical theme later shows up in the ritual of the full moon in which either a wand or dagger is lowered into a chalice. This is known as the Great Rite, which is intended to merge the divine feminine and divine masculine into one. The oldest form of this practice involved a piece of antler and a gourd. This is covered in chapter 5 on the old rites of Witchcraft.

It is from the Grain Mysteries that the ritual use of flour arises, and its white nature is tied to the moon. We catch a glimpse of this concept in some old folklore about flour and the Sabbat. In the associated lore, the grain growing on a plant absorbed the chthonic nature of the Underworld through its roots, and the Celestial Mysteries through flying insects landing on the tips of the grain while still on the stock. The classic example is of fireflies landing on the grain on the night of the summer solstice, which was frequently seen in Italy. Folklore evolved that the fireflies were actually faeries. In this way, the grain took on additional mystical properties.

In Charles Leland's research on Italian Witchcraft, he writes about the Witches' Sabbat meal. Flour is made into a meal for the celebration with the belief that eating the grain imparts the secrets of other worlds. In essence, this Sabbat meal is the moon wisdom absorbed into the grain. The moon is seen to go down into the Underworld in the west after traveling in the celestial night from the east. In this way, it carries the gathered secrets as well. In the Sabbat meal small white round cakes that resemble the full moon are used, and this became the idea of a communion meal with the moon and its associated spirits.

A popular text in the 1960s was known as the Charge of the Goddess. One segment of it, drawn from Leland's book *Aradia: Or the Gospel of the Witches,* reads:

Once a month, when the moon is full

You must come to a lonely place

In a forest all together

And adore the powerful spirit of my mother Diana,

And whomever would like to learn Witchcraft

Who will not surpass her,

My mother will teach them all things[2]

This is part of the theme of enlightenment beneath the moon. All of this points to the power of night, the "lonely place," and the moonlit forest. These are all components of the awakening and the sustaining of Witchery. Here the Witch is bathed in the mystical light of the moon, an ancient connection to every Witch of the past. For this is the same moon that our ancestors gazed upon; it is not a symbol. Therefore, it is the one timeless, enduring connection still available to us; it is the past and present shining down upon us. This joins all Witches together in time and space.

Now that have we explored the night nature of the Witch, let us turn to the process of rousing the Witch within us.

---

2 Charles G. Leland, *Aradia: Or the Gospel of the Witches,* trans. Mario Pazzaglini and Dina Pazzaglini (Blaine, WA: Phoenix Publishing, 1999).

THE WITCHENING

In this section I present a step-by-step order, method by method, that will establish the essential foundation for the practices of Witchery. It is the oldest material from the 1960s scene that I possess, and it is not fragmented. Back in the day, it was reportedly only given to initiates.

The following is a process by which you can connect with the forces of Old Magic, and from which you can draw and raise power. This section will provide you with the connections to the chthonic, terrestrial, and celestial alignments from which you will draw in your practice of Witchery.

There are five steps in establishing the Witchening, and together they will empower you in the practice of Witchcraft:

1. Gathering the Virtue of the Moon
2. Meeting the Wafting
3. Aligning the Witch's Blade
4. Creating the Witch's Pentacle
5. Making the Witch's Ring

Once each of these steps is completed, you will possess the quintessence of witchery. This quality will be what you draw upon later for every ritual or work of magic. This is true even if you are not intentionally aware of the quintessence at any give time. A Witch is a Witch at all times, and Old Witchery always accompanies the Witch from moment to moment.

Step One: Gathering the Virtue of the Moon

We will begin with the Rooted Ways connection, which involves using a candle and saying specific words. When training begins, the candle is lit and set at the feet of the student. He or she can be standing or seated.

The teacher cups her or his hands safely around the candle flame and says to the student,

"There is a light

That the eye cannot see.

I pass part of it to you

As it was first passed to me."

Next, the teacher slowly moves the candle up to the head of the student while saying the following words:

"From feet to head,

I pass the light

Of what can be known

But in the night."

At this point, the student takes the candle as the teacher continues.

"One comes now

To one who's been

The ways of old

Pass once again."

The candle is set to the side and the first session begins.

The moon virtue symbol contains three chevrons stacked under a circle.

It is here that we need to talk about the occult concept in Witchcraft known as *virtue*. This is not about anything of a moral nature. Instead, it is defined as a beneficial quality or the power of a thing. In the Rooted Ways, as the starting point, we draw the virtue of the moon to us. This involves the use of an ancient symbol called a chevron, which is basically a V shape. It appears in prehistoric art associated with the divine feminine.

Receiving the virtue of the moon takes place on the night of the full moon. The moon must be seen without anything obstructing your view. You will be forming the chevron with both hands, using this gesture to draw the moon virtue to yourself. To form the hands, press both wrists together and then outwardly extend the open palms to the left and right. This will create the chevron shape.

Kneel, and with the chevron hand posture, lift your hands up slightly above your head so that the full moon appears cupped between your palms. Spend a moment looking at the moon and its light. Note any halo or corona that may appear. You want to connect to the moon as ancient and sacred. Remember that this moon is the exact same one that every Witch from the past once looked upon. Affirm it by saying,

> *"Here I look upon the same moon that did every Witch before me, and beneath which every invocation was spoken.*

I cradle the timeless connection, and I am one with the ancient wonder of this mystical orb."

When you feel ready to proceed, say these words as you lower the chevron downward:

"The same moon the ancestors beheld in the night,

I kneel beneath now and receive of its light.

In me the past, present, and future unite."

Pause at your forehead, and then move the chevron to your heart. At this point, collapse the chevron by pressing your palms together. Next, place the palm of the right hand over the back of the left hand, and then press the hands gently on your heart. In doing so, you are embedding the virtue of the moon within your body. To complete this phase, spend a few minutes looking at the moon and be receptive to any communication or feeling.

The key thing to know is that virtue is an energy that keeps you connected to its source. It is also the energy that is the Witchery within you. Its resonance distinguishes you from other types of magic users and occult practitioners. All the Witchery you do in the future will be empowered or blessed by the virtue that resonates within you from the moon's virtue. Imbuing every spell, ritual, or work of magic with it is always the first act of the Witch. See chapter 5 on Old Magic for details on the prescribed method.

Step Two: Meeting the Wafting

Now that you carry the moon's virtue, you will be able to sense and connect with what is called the waft of night. It is an occult energy that is part of the nature of night itself in the Witch's world. This energy is generated by night and rests upon the tree branches, much like the morning dew coats the grass. Once sensed, it can be gathered up by the Witch.

The waft is what might be called a "pre-sentient" quality. It is primal by nature, and it holds in place the old memory of the forest, which existed before contamination by the "evolution" of humankind. It is pure and raw; it is untamed. Our ancestors felt its presence long ago when they were forest dwellers. It wafted from the trees, and it bestowed a sense of the mystical world. Something unseen was passing from the trees and making itself known to those with occult awareness. A communication of some type was taking place in the soft blackness of night.

The Witch connects with the wafting to generate an energy field of origin. Origin is the state of the beginning, a return to a time when humans lived in common cause with nature. It was a time of the Old Magic. When the waft is set in motion, the Witch creates the foundation of procreation, a pure energy untainted by any and all concepts before it or in the present. From this anything the Witch can manifest can arise, and nothing contaminates it from outside forces. This is important because one's magic can be mutated by thought-forms that lose their integrity. The waft holds all in place.

It is a practice in the Rooted Ways to evoke the waft before any ritual, spell casting, work of magic, divination, or act of healing. The method of connecting to the waft begins with finding a setting where trees are present and close together. Ideally, you will want trees whose branches are fairly visible through the foliage. The trees should be at least fifty feet away from you.

On the night of the full moon, place yourself in a position where the moon appears above the tree branches. Focus your eyes on the upper tips of the branches, and allow your vision to blur slightly. Hold this for a few moments and try to feel a presence in the trees.

If you are receptive, then this should happen in little time. When you feel connected, and ready, make the following sound (slowly in a whisper) while looking at the branches in the moonlight:

"Eee—oh . . . may . . . kee . . . ahs

Eee . . . oh . . . may . . . kee . . . ahs

Eee . . . oh . . . may . . . kee . . . ahs"

This will awaken the waft, and it will take note of you. This sound will then be your word of power for evoking or invoking the waft. It must always be whispered. Evoking the waft before any ritual or work of magic will create the occult ambiance. Never utter the sounds in any mundane setting. Only use it in a ritual or magical setting (otherwise you will negate its effectiveness, render it mundane, and it will then withdraw from its connection to you).

Now let us look at one different practical use of drawing the waft. Here it is important to note that the waft awakens from its pre-sentient passive state only when it is "observed" (at which point it merges with your consciousness). This creates a shared consciousness. You give it intent or purpose through your desire to manifest an outcome.

Bear in mind that the waft is procreative energy, a raw source that responds to being informed. This means that it receives your focused intention and your thoughts, and makes them a cohesive force for magic. To accomplish this, you will need to be clear in your mind what it is you want to achieve. Perhaps it is opening a portal in your ritual work or casting a spell for prosperity. Whatever it is, draw a relevant symbol to represent it. For example, a spiral can represent a portal, and a dollar sign can symbolize prosperity. Once drawn, beneath the symbol write the pertinent word that is the core intent of your work to be done. Looking at the symbol, repeat its meaning out loud three times. Here is an example using the idea of a portal:

> *"This spiral represents the opening to the spirit world and grants me access."*

Once the waft is evoked through the calling sounds, look at the symbol. This will impregnate the gathered waft with your intention. It will cause the waft to imbue your work with your intention. This is different from simply calling the waft to create an occult ambiance. The former is a vibration of energy that aligns you with the ancient mindset of Witchcraft. The latter is your imprint on this energy. You are giving it a formed thought of your own, and it will in turn pass this into the ritual or magical work. In contrast, simply calling the waft without imbuing it will establish the ancient essence of Witchery itself. The call establishes the presence of full potentiality, while the formed thought creates a finite purpose under the direction of the Witch.

Step Three: Aligning the Witch's Blade

The dagger (often called the athame) is a tool of high value in the Arts of Witchery. In the Rooted Ways, the dagger is a double-edged steel blade with a black wooden handle. The double-edged blade represents the material and nonmaterial realities, and its ability to slice between them. The pointed tip of the blade signifies the sacred star and therefore symbolizes the celestial connection. The hilt symbolizes the earth. The color black on the handle represents night, and the wood symbolizes the black night of the woods (a primal connection).

To charge the dagger, go outside on the night of the black moon (when no crescent is seen). To prepare the setting, using white flour, mark a triangle on the ground. It needs to be at least the size of your

The Witch's blade, also known as an athame or dagger, is usually made of double-edged steel and natural or stained black wood.

hand. You will also need a pitcher of fresh water. The flour represents the Grain Mysteries, which tell us that the roots of plants absorb energy from the Underworld and thereby possess the secrets of that realm. In the following magical operation, you will be uniting the Celestial Mysteries (from starlight) with the Underworld Mysteries (held in the blackness beneath the soil).

Hold the blade upright to the brightest star you can find in the night sky. Orient the tip of the blade so that it seems to touch the lower half of the star. Mentally connect with the star sitting on the tip of the dagger. When you are ready, speak these words:

"Starlight set upon the blade,

As of ancient times in misty glade,

I draw you now as starry fire,

To aid this Witch as I desire."

As you focus on the tip of the blade, slowly lower the dagger (keeping your gaze upon the tip). Move the dagger from your head down to the genital area. Point the tip of the blade downward and say:

"Star seed above,

star seed below.

Light into the blackness go.

Mysteries are joined,

and there all set aglow."

At this point, kneel on the ground. Push the blade down into the soil directly in the center of the triangle, all the way to the hilt. Next, place your palms on each side of the blade and say:

"Watchers in the blackness, who gather in silence when secret mysteries are performed, I evoke you.

Night, faithful keeper of my secrets, and stars who, together with the moon, dissolve away the light of day, I evoke you.

Daughters of Night, the three faces, who know all my designs, and come to help the incantations and the craft of the Witches, I evoke you.

Earth, who furnishes witches with powerful herbs, and all the breezes, winds, mountains, rivers, and lakes, and all the gods of the groves and all the gods of the night, be present to help me.

Night-wandering queen, and lord of the shadowed wooded places, I evoke you.

I bid all to look with favor now upon this undertaking."

Next, place your right hand firmly over your left on the handle and concentrate upon the dagger. Imagine it glowing with light. Then, pour the pitcher of water over the triangle of flour. This will merge the celestial and terrestrial forces.

After a few minutes, remove the dagger from the soil and clean it off with a white cloth. The next step is to imbue the dagger with a magical charge. To do this you will need a lodestone (magnet), a flaming candle, and a bowl of fresh water.

Begin by heating the blade in the candle flame for a couple of minutes. This awakens the memory of the creative force of fire that first forged the blade. Once the blade is quite hot, say these words:

"Blade of steel,

Your charge shall be

To banish all I bid of Thee!"

Then immediately plunge the blade into the bowl of water. If heated properly, you will hear a hissing sound as hot metal meets cold water. This seals the magical intent into the knife and records the memory. Afterward, thoroughly dry off the blade.

To complete the process, you will need to magnetize the blade. Take a medium size lodestone and stroke it against the blade from the tip down to the hilt. Do not stroke back and forth, but always in one direction, firmly and moderately, nine times on each side of the blade.

Repeat the process again: nine times on the first side of the blade, and then the opposite. As you stroke the magnet along the blade, periodically say these words:

"Blade of steel,

Your charge shall be

To attract all things I bid of Thee!"

The final process for charging the knife is to connect it with the forces of above, below, and in-between. Begin by presenting the blade, holding it upward to the stars, and say:

"I am a Witch,

Kindred one of the night.

Stars above bear witness."

Next, place the tip of the dagger into the soil and say:

"Starlight, starfire, I join you with the forces below."

Push the blade down into the soil and say:

"Earth below, be mated with light."

After a few moments, remove the knife from the soil and press the flat side of the blade (horizontal) against your solar plexus. Say:

"I join you with star and earth. I meet the forces in-between."

You can now clean the knife, wrap it in a cloth, and take it with you. (Note: To place a lunar charge on the blade, see chapter 5.)

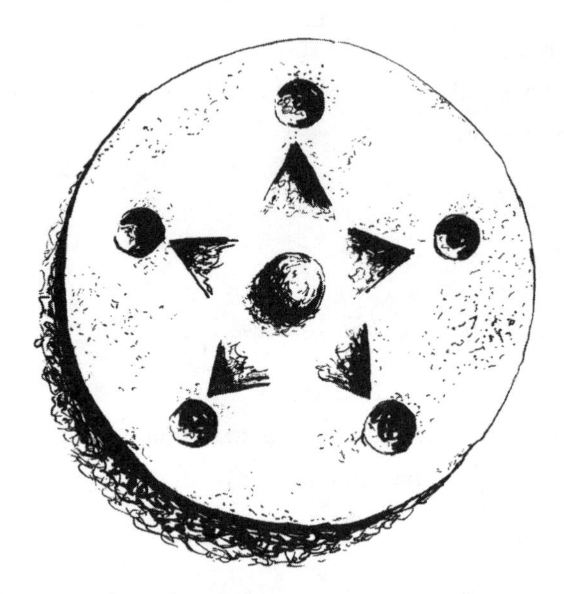

The pentacle is the chthonic connection that joins the Witch to the Spirit of the Land, the ancestors, and the unseen world—the rooted places.

Step Four: Creating the Witch's Pentacle

In the Rooted Ways, we use a clay pentacle that is buried in the earth. It is the chthonic connection that joins the Witch to the Spirit of the Land, the ancestors, and the unseen world—the rooted places. One of its names is the shadow disk. This is not to be confused with the Witch's altar pentacle, which represents the elemental tool of earth.

Before making the shadow disk pentacle, you will need to select three small stones of the same kind. I use tiger eye, but any stone that bears meaning for you is fine. One stone is designated for the pentacle, one for the Witch's ring, and one for the altar stone. Have these ready before creating the pentacle. You will also need either bakeable clay or a type of clay that dries permanently. (It is going to be buried, so you do not want it to be dissolved by the elements.)

With the clay in hand, roll it smooth and flat. One of your small stones will be set into the clay, so you will need to make the pentacle thick enough for the stone to be pushed halfway down into it. Beyond being able to accommodate this stone, the thickness of the pentacle is not significant.

Next, cut a circle out of the clay to serve as your pentacle. You can press a bowl into the clay to ensure a perfect circle. If you do this, make sure to oil the rim of the bowl so that the clay does not stick to it. The size of the pentacle should be 8 to 12 inches wide.

When the round pentacle is ready to work with, press your index finger around the inside edges as appears in the illustration.

This will connect you, through your hand, to the pentacle. The meaning and power of this will show itself shortly. Next, using the tip of your Witch's blade, make a V on the inner field of the pentacle as shown in the illustration (page 28) by pressing the tip into the clay. This is the chevron symbol, the mark of the moon that will connect it to the celestial emanation. Lastly, set a small stone directly in the center of the pentacle. The stone will hold the magic in place and will resonate with the other two stones, and from this combination you will have the trine Witchery.

The trine refers to one third of a circle, which is 120 degrees. It also refers to cooperation, as in the astrological meaning of a planet in trine with another. In the trine of Witchery, the three stones form an etheric field or sphere around the Witch. This places the Witch in an interactive energy that completes the occult circuit from which the Witch draws power.

Once everything is in place on the pentacle's surface, allow it to dry thoroughly. (You can leave it out under the moon and through the day.) Then, on the night of a full moon, bury it in a spot to which you can easily return. Make sure the symbolism is facing upright.

In the future, you will be offering libations from your rituals over the buried pentacle. You will place the palm of your hand over the buried pentacle to swear oaths and to call forth Underworld forces. Another function is to place the wand upright over the area and call upon the goddess Hecate. Oaths given in this way are very ancient and powerful. You will find more on all of this in chapter 5.

The hand has long been associated with holding and grasping the mystical. We can see this in the art of palmistry, in which the lines of the hands indicate various traits and lifetime outcomes. In the occult arts we see statues of hands as well as symbolic drawings of them. Setting the hand over the buried pentacle puts the Witch in the in-between place, in the middle of above and below. This completes the occult circuit, and the celestial and terrestrial energies flow through the Witch.

Step Five: Making the Witch's Ring

The final and perhaps most important alignment tool is the Witch's ring. The ring brings the circle of the quintessence to the command of the Witch. The ring bears the second stone and is carried by the Witch. This is in contrast to the stationary stones, one set in the clay pentacle and the other on the altar. The mobile nature of the ring allows the Witch to extend the influences and emanations that arise from the pentacle and altar stones.

The role of the altar stone is to maintain the resonance of sacredness. This is akin to the stone in the pentacle that also resonates with the Spirit of the Land. These connections back to the Witch, through the three stones, empower the Witch in key ways. There is, at the core, the metaphysical principle of the three worlds: above, below and in-between. The pentacle stone represents the world below, the altar stone symbolizes the divine world above, and the ring moves between the worlds along with the Witch.

If you can make your own ring, or have someone else do so, this is ideal for customizing it. If not, select a ring that already has the type of stone used for the pentacle and altar. This will complete the trine. In considering a ring, silver is the preferred metal, as it is lunar in nature.

Once you have the ring, follow this procedure. On the night of the full moon, at 9 p.m. or midnight, empower the ring with the four creative elemental natures: earth, air, fire, and water. This requires four bowls, each denoting one of the four sacred directions of north, east, south, and west. The north bowl will contain fresh soil or pebbles; the east bowl some smoking incense; the south bowl a lighted red votive candle; and the west bowl fresh water.

Beginning with the south bowl, pass the ring safely through the candle flame three times, each time saying:

> *"Spirit of fire, imbue this ring with your force of transformation."*

Visualize flames darting in and out of the ring.

Next, pass the ring through the incense smoke three times, each time saying:

> *"Spirit of air, imbue this ring with your mystical unseen nature."*

Visualize the ring disappearing and reappearing.

Now dip the ring into the water three times, each time saying:

> *"Spirit of water, imbue this ring with your nature of cleansing and flow."*

Visualize the ring cresting like a wave and then crashing down.

Conclude the elemental charge by tapping the ring on the soil/pebbles three times, each time saying:

> *"Spirit of earth, imbue this ring with your binding and enduring nature."*

Visualize the ring appearing like the towering wall encircling a castle.

Pick the ring up with the left hand and extend it to the moon. Use your left eye to look through the opening of the band so that you can see the moon encircled. Then speak the words of enchantment:

"By fire, air, water, and earth,

Now the Witch's ring is birthed.

Here below in this moonlit hour

Awakens now the timeless power."

Next, present the ring to the four directional quarters of north, east, south, and west, saying:

"By the forces and spirits of earth, air, water, and fire,

Be this manifest as the Witch's ring of power."

Your ring is now manifest, and ready to be charged with a specific protection spell. Details for doing this can be found in chapter 5.

SUMMARY OF THE QUINTESSENCE

Now that the five aspects of Witchery have been presented, let us review their vital role. Virtue is the first to be drawn because it sets the resonance of the Witch; with this occult magnetism in place all other things can be attracted. The virtue of the moon permeates the aura of the body and keeps the Witch in the stream of lunar emanation. In this light the Witch is intimately connected with all that is associated with the moon.

When we possess the energy within us that we call "the virtue of the moon," we can then see the mystical waft on the treetops. This is because virtue bestows mystical sight, which allows the Witch to sense nonmaterial reality. It is the virtue of the moon that is the basis for the saying that Witches recognize their own. The role of virtue is to imbue the Witch with a lunar vibration that intimately links her or him to the spirits, entities, and goddess of the moon (and its sphere of influence).

The next concept to follow in order of the five components is the waft. It is the idea of the night's mystical energy caught and held by tree branches. The presence of the waft heightens the preexisting consciousness of the trees and therefore merges the forest and woodlands with the Otherworld. The waft is the mystical, etheric essence that sustains the enchanted world within material reality. It is, in a certain sense, much like the soul that enlivens the material body. Without this, there is only the mundane, the material form. Such forms come and go in their time, but the waft is timeless and enduring. The role of the waft is to draw enchantment to the Witch as an energy that can be used for ritual and magic. The waft is also the fabric that weaves the virtue of the moon into the Witch. It is a presence that connects the Witch with the mystical realm. Do you now see the importance of the relationship between virtue, waft, and the Witch in a beneficial way?

Continuing on, we now turn our attention to the Witch's dagger. This is a unique tool that is both terrestrial and celestial in nature. The tip of the blade is star-blessed and gleams with starlight. Upon it rests the star seed, an important element in the Witch's magic (more on that in chapter 5).

The primary role of the Witch's blade is to slice through the barrier between the material and nonmaterial realms. These are sometimes called the mortal realm and the spirit realm. In effect, the blade penetrates that which separates the dimensions. As a result, the Witch has access to a corridor between the worlds. Once the Witch enters into that place, she or he is not subject to the limitations or rules of either realm. This is where the Witch's magic prevails in accord with her or his abilities. In chapter 5 you will find various methods of using the Witch's blade. For now, envision that when you hold the wooden handle you are connected to the Spirit of the Land through the Sacred Tree of the Grove. When you lift the blade, you draw the power of the Great Beloved Star (what today is known as Venus). When you point the blade down, you part the heavens and the earth, opening the mystical corridor.

We turn now to the clay pentacle. By pressing the tip of the Witch's blade into the clay pentacle, you formed a five-pointed star comprised of five chevron marks. This plants the star seed into the clay, and through this magical act the clay is impregnated with the celestial. It will bring stars to the Underworld, and, "as above, so below," with blade in hand, you will stand in the in-between places.

Once constructed, the pentacle connects the celestial with the terrestrial. In ancient myth the Underworld was illuminated, and by some accounts the light came from stars in the cavern of the Underworld. The Witch's pentacle imbeds the star beneath the earth. It is a light that displaces darkness. When libations are poured on the ground above the pentacle, the spirits of the dead below are vitalized. They are drawn to the pentacle, especially those of your blood lineage. This is because the fluids remind them of the blood that flows in life. Witches have long been associated with the ability to communicate with the dead.

Placing the left palm on the pentacle zone connects the Witch to her or his ancestors through the fingerprints on the buried pentacle. The stone on the pentacle joins energetically with the stone on the ring worn by the Witch. The two stones, in turn, connect with the stone on the altar. This places the Witch inside a sphere of energy that is comprised of earth, stars, and divinity. It is a moment of return to the origin, a time when our ancestors reached out to the enchanted world. In this they were open to the Mysteries, and the Mysteries flowed to them in return.

The final piece of the quintessence is the Witch's ring. The ring is the centerpiece that brings everything together in terms of the Witch's access to power through the quintessence. There are two primary purposes for the ring: alignment and protection. The alignments are to the forces emanating from the celestial and the terrestrial. Protection includes imbedding a flaming blue star within the ring's stone, which can be drawn out as needed. You will find more on this in chapter 5.

Looking at the quintessence as a whole, we see the foundational elements of Witchery. The moon bestows the magic of its spiritual virtue to the Witch. The tree branches hold and offer the mystical waft of occult energy that invokes an Otherworld nature to the Witch. Next, we find the Witch's blade, a tool that parts and opens the mortal and spirit realms. The pentacle connects the three worlds of ancient thought: above, below, and in-between. Through this the Witch is the pillar at the crossroads, and she or he is the conduit for the flow of mystical and magical currents. Lastly, the ring draws them all together under the direction of the Witch. It is the Witch's center of the Arts of Witchery.

CHAPTER TWO

THE MYSTICAL AND THE SACRED

In the progress of the witch four comprehensive stages are noticeable. She was in the beginning the counsellor and consoler of man, the genius of the domestic arts, the treasury of knowledge, and the inspiration of belief. She was the prophet, priest, and king of paganism, and her territory was the world.

—IAN FERGUSON, *THE PHILOSOPHY OF WITCHCRAFT*

While it is not uncommon to think of Witchcraft as solely a practice, to many it is also a religion or spiritual path. The idea of veneration or worship continues on into the Christian era with accusations that Witches "worship" the devil. It is noteworthy that the underlying religious tone is never absent in the writings on Witches and Witchcraft of any given century.

In the Rooted Ways there is a foundational and core presence of the mystical and the spiritual. These shaped the ways of Witchcraft and underlie the various practices, beliefs, symbols, and tools of Witchcraft as a system.

Long ago our ancestors were forest dwellers, and this influenced the development of the mindset within the practitioners of Witchcraft. Such a lifestyle set the tone for an enchanted worldview. One example lies in the canopy of branches overhead. This suggested a demarcation between the human world and the heavens. A person could climb the trees to the top and stand between the two worlds. Here we can see the ancient concept of the worlds: above, below, and in-between. As was noted earlier, the goddess Hecate ruled over the three worlds, and she was also the goddess of Witchcraft.

It is said that the ways of Witchcraft were spirit-taught to those humans who were receptive and perhaps even predisposed in some way to practice the Arts. While some humans were hunters, toolmakers, builders, and so on, there were others who were proficient at hearing the voices of spirits. These were the first people to become Witches. In turn they taught other people, and over time a system developed. This process eventually became formalized into a rite of initiation. It is, however, important to note that all of this ultimately originated from the Greenwood realm of nature.

THE WITCH AND THE FOREST

We know from various sources that our ancestors venerated or worshipped trees. This type of practice must stretch back to something less formalized; perhaps it is a sensing of an inner communication deep within. Myths and legends are filled with stories of magical forests and enchanted woods. Evolving from ancient practices that are naturally connected to forests we find the maypole, the Yule log, and what is now called the Christmas tree.

Some of the old tales feature beings attached to trees; among the most famous are the dryads, or wood nymphs. Other stories reveal that gods inhabited trees, and there are tales of gods suspended from trees, for example, Odin, who hung upside down from a tree until he gained enlightenment. In mystical Christianity, Jesus is suspended upon a tree in the form of a cross through which he demonstrates the power of self-sacrifice. It is an ancient theme in various cultures. All of these themes point to the idea of consciousness associated with trees in one way or another.

Mystic and poet William Sharp (who wrote under the pen name Fiona Macleod) portrayed the consciousness of the forest in his writing

Where the Forest Murmurs. He speaks of becoming aware of something communicating within the forest itself:

> *Something is now evident, that was not evident: [it] is entered into the forest. The leaves know it: the bracken knows it: the secret is in every copse, in every thicket, is palpable in every glade, is abroad in every shadow-thridden avenue, is common to the spreading bough and the leaning branch. It is not a rumour; for that might be the wind stealthily lifting his long wings from glade to glade. It is not a whisper; for that might be the secret passage of unquiet airs, furtive heralds of the unloosening thunder. It is not a sigh; for that might be the breath of branch and bough, of fern-frond and grass, obvious in the great suspense. It is an ineffable communication. It comes along the ways of silence; along the ways of sound: its light feet are on sunrays and on shadows. Like dew, one knows not whether it's mysteriously gathered from below or secretly come from on high: simply it is there, above, around, beneath.*[1]

Sharp goes on to depict the woodpecker as an agent of the forest that awakens it, keeps it mindful lest the trees fall into slumber. In this light, the woodpecker moves from tree to tree as it senses one withdrawing from its connection to the forest. It then rouses the tree with its hammering beak. Sharp points out that the ancient Italic god Picus (father of the woodland god, Faunus) is associated with the woodpecker. The earliest depiction of Picus shows him as a wooden pillar mounted with a woodpecker. In Ovid's *Metamorphoses*, Book XIV, the Witch Circe is responsible for Picus taking on the form of a woodpecker. This raises the ancient thought that the Witch is connected to the idea of embracing the forest as something sentient (and of maintaining it).

---

1 Fiona Macleod, *Where the Forest Murmurs: Nature Essays* (London: Country Life and George Newnes, 1906), 4.

The tree as a gateway is an ancient theme. Sometimes the tree is portrayed as a birthing womb. The ancient Greek writer Virgil writes in book VIII of *The Aeneid*,

"These woods were the first seat of sylvan powers,

Of nymphs, and fauns, and savage men who took

Their birth from trunks of trees and stubborn oak . . ."[2]

In the *Odyssey*, the hero is challenged to present his lineage and to distinguish himself from those who "in times of old" were "born of oak or rock." The ancient writer Hesiod states that Zeus made "the brazen race of men" out of ash trees. In northern Europe, we find the great ash tree known as Yggdrasil, from which all things (including humans) were created.

Historian Mircea Eliade, in his book *Patterns in Comparative Religion*, writes of the mystical bond between trees and humans. He presents the ancient view that the souls of our ancestors reside in the trees. Eliade also explores the old customs of people marrying trees, and the presence of a tree in rites of initiation. He brings up an interesting concept that humans are "an ephemeral appearance of a new plant modality." Eliade goes on to say that when some human dies, she or he returns as a seed to the tree and enters it in spirit form. In doing so, humans become "one with the womb of all things." In this light, "death is a renewal of contact with the source of all life." Eliade writes of this theme being widespread: "The belief that the souls of ancestors are in some way attached to certain trees from which they pass as embryos into women's wombs form a compact group with a great many variations."[3]

---

2 Virgil, *The Aeneid*, trans. John Dryden (London: George Routledge and Sons, 1887), 191.

3 Mircea Eliade, *Patterns in Comparative Religion*, trans. Rosemary Sheed (Lincoln: University of Nebraska Press, 1996).

The concept of the tree as a womb-gate or a doorway between the worlds is tied to the theme of the white tree mythos in Old World Witchcraft. The theme involves the white birch and Spirits of the Dead. Early tales of faery lore (in what is now Italy) seem to suggest that spirits of the dead could become faeries. There's some speculation that the concept of faery mounds evolved from the construction of Neolithic burial mounds, which were made with a single hole in them to allow the soul to enter and exit at will.

In the Ash, Birch and Willow tradition of Witchcraft, the white tree stands at the in-between place where the material world and the spirit world meet. On the "faery side" of the tree, the tree is a shimmering white light; and on the "mortal side" it is a physical birch tree. From a mystical perspective, faeries use the white tree as a doorway to and from the mortal realm. Souls of the Dead are envisioned as passing through the tree into the Otherworld. Associated tales portray the faery world as being just above the land of the Dead, and that souls pass through the faery realm on their journey.

Among the oldest references to Witches, we find a connection to the dead and the realm of the Dead. One example is the tale of Circe, who shows a group of Greek heroes the way to the Underworld and instructs them on how to communicate with the dead. Various tales about the Witch Medea depict her as using a cauldron and her magic to control life and death. Dominican preacher Jacopo Passavanti, in his work *The Mirror of True Repentance*, wrote that some people accompany Witches to secret night gatherings (Sabbats) to receive communication from deceased loved ones.[4]

Old Italian Witch lore features a walnut tree as the meeting place of Witches in the area of Benevento. This theme is in the same class as the Walpurgis gatherings of Witches in the Brocken, the peak in

4 Walter Stevens, *Demon Lovers: Witchcraft, Sex, and the Crisis of Belief* (Chicago: University of Chicago Press, 2002), 132.

the Harz Mountains of Germany. The walnut tree of Benevento had long been the site of serpent veneration, and in ancient Roman times the serpent was associated with the ancestral spirit. It is featured on ancestral shrines known as the *lararium*, which bore images of the lare spirits, who were guardians of family bloodlines.

In the lore of the walnut of Benevento, it is said that the tree existed as long as memory could tell. Its foliage was reportedly so dense that the shade beneath the tree's branches was as black as night. Legend has it that Witches gathered there for countless centuries. Then in the seventh century, St. Barbato had the tree cut down in his attempt to Christianize the city of Benevento. The memory of the tree, however, never disappeared over the following centuries. It remains one of the few trees specifically mentioned as an ally of Witches and one at which they gathered.

The unnamed sacred tree in the grove of the goddess Diana at Lake Nemi can be added to this general theme, if we allow that she was a goddess associated with Witchcraft. This does seem to be supported by writers such as the ancient Roman Horace, who in "The Witch's Incantation" depicts Diana as being present during the secret rites of Witches, and who bears witness to those rituals.

Charles Leland referred to Diana as "Queen of the Fairies," and faeries are associated with walnuts in Italian lore. In some stories, a helper faery comes forth from a walnut to aid someone in the tale. At other times, the walnut opens to produce the needed thing in a quest, and all of this is under the domain of the faery. But this is all surface lore, and behind it is something much older.

In folklore, we find trees having doorways or portals, which most often appear as a hollow in the tree. Entering the hollow leads the seeker into various realms, one of which is the land of faeries. This is not unlike the theme of fairy mounds found in various regions and lands. On a more primal level, this idea is linked to connections that empower and vitalize the Witch.

Recent scientific research indicates that trees communicate with one another through a linked system of extended roots. Fungus on the forest floor joins the root network, acting much like neurotransmitters in the human brain. This is somewhat reminiscent of the theme in the movie *Avatar*. Biologists such as Rupert Sheldrake are demonstrating that trees communicate with each other through chemicals released from their leaves, which are spread to the forest through the air. In this sense, we see part of the mind of the forest at work.

The entangled roots and the leafy branches restore us to our ancestral home in the forest. The old god of Witchcraft—He of the Deep Wooded Places—manifests to the Witch who enters the forest in the remembered ways. Witches once gathered in the woods not to hide but to dance with life and death. The old gods are light and blackness; they are awakened by the drumming of feet on the forest floor that sound to the roots below.

They speak to the Witch through the branches, and in the boughs the Witch sees the patterns of the limbs that form the ancient runes. It is the language of Verdanta, the *knowing* that encircles the Witch from the verdant woodland messengers. Everything that the Witch receives from the forest is imbued with the memory of shadow, the organic memory of the earth. Into the hands of the Witch is passed the leafy grimoire written by seed, stem, bud, leaf, and flower.

In some of the ancient myths, maidens are turned into trees to save them from unwanted suitors. In other myths, people are turned into trees to bind their actions or to punish them for their wrongs. Still other legends tell of trees that prevent access or that fend off foes. These are all the outer layers of exoteric tales covering the underlying esoteric mysteries.

The Witch carries the wand of the Greenwood magic, the scepter of gnosis, before which all veneers dissolve away. Legends fall back into myth, and myth then crumbles away to expose the ancient forgotten time. It is then that the mists part, and the Witch emerges from the thickets and is seen once again in the deep wooded places.

WITCHES AS THE PLANT PEOPLE OF OLD EUROPE

Ancient writings depict the Witch as living among the herb-clad hills. This idea is connected to the long-standing theme of the traditional plants of Witchcraft. The oldest word in Western culture to be translated into modern English as Witch is the ancient Greek *Pharmakis* (*far-mah-kiss*). Over time, with the blend of magic and herbalism, the Witch came to be known as *Pharmakeute* (pronounced *far-mah-koo-tay*).

Historian Richard Gordon commented that the earliest example in extant Greek of the word *pharmakis* became one of the standard words for wise woman/witch.[5] Our modern words *pharmacy* and *pharmacist* are derived from the same etymology. In ancient times, all medicine came from plants (sometimes mixed with animal parts). The fact that a Witch was called a Pharmakeute demonstrates the ancient connection between the Witch and plants.

The knowledge of chemicals came much later than the appearance of the ancient Pharmakeute/Witch. Our most distant ancestors believed that intoxication was the result of possession by spirits. In other words, the spirit of the vine made a person drunk, or the spirit of a plant wielded power over whoever ingested an herbal potion. In this light, we can see a type of spiritual tradition, one focused on a relationship between plant spirits and the Witch/Pharmakeute (as opposed to

---

5 Richard Gordon, "Imagining Greek and Roman Magic," in *Witchcraft and Magic in Europe, Volume 2: Ancient Greece and Rome*, ed. Bengt Ankarloo and Stuart Clark (Philadelphia: University of Pennsylvania Press, 1999), 251.

the applied science of botany or alchemy). Therefore, in this chapter, we view the Pharmakeute as one in relationship with spirits and entities of the plant realm.

As previously mentioned, our ideas about magic, spirits, and other realms may well have been wired by the ancestral experience of living in the forest. This was a realm in which there was no horizon, only a depth of endless trees. Above was the canopy of branches that seemingly demarcated the world from the sky. It spoke to one place in which humankind dwelled and another that contained the sun, moon, and stars. All of this was seen through a visible barrier.

In the deep wooded places were shadow and the sounds of things stirring and moving about, all of which was unseen. These experiences may have been regarded as spirits moving in the thickets. In some areas of dense growth, openings could be seen that resembled archways or corridors (suggesting entrances into another world beyond that of mortal kind). For our ancestors, this might well have stimulated ideas that became their enchanted worldview and from which much of the old lore may be traced. This explanation, however, does not dismiss the reality of the other realms and invisible spirits. Instead, the lore can be regarded as the means through which this worldview was communicated to primitive humans.

Mystical communication requires interpretation, and one of the surest methods is to have skilled interpreters. They have had many titles over the centuries: shaman, sorcerer, mystic, wizard, necromancer, Witch. In old lore, such practitioners possess a wand or staff (tools of the Greenwood) and an ally from the Otherworld. Often this ally is an animal, but in older times it was a plant—or, more accurately, a plant spirit. This is why the etymology of the earliest word used for Witchcraft points to plants.

This relationship between the Witch and the spirits of plants developed in the forest of our distant ancestors. In many old legends, and in a number of faery tales, the Witch lives in the forest or in a cottage in the woods. The Witch remains in the primal or untamed world not as a rejection of civilization but because she or he chooses to stay connected to the ancestral current that flows from our original home in the forest. There, in the deep wooded places, the Witch is one with the Greenwood and its magic. Part of that magic is connected to the vast network of roots that spread beneath the land. Through them, plants tap deeply into the organic memory of the earth (into which the essence of all living things has been absorbed over untold ages). The Witch, in turn, taps into the spirit of the plant and calls forth the ancient memories that sleep below.

Many plant spirits assist the Pharmakeute, who remains true to the relationship. In the Ash, Birch and Willow system of Old Witchery, aiding the Witch is a powerful entity known as She of the Thorn-Blooded Rose. The deepest secrets of the Greenwood are protected by what the rose symbolizes in old Mystery Traditions. The term *sub rosa,* which means "to keep silent," originates from the inner teachings of the rose. Oaths are sworn before the thorns of the rose, and a blood covenant is established.

Deep within the earth rests the organic memory of all who have lived and died upon our planet. This is called shadow and can be thought of as the organic counterpart to the Akashic records in Eastern mysticism. Within shadow is nature's memory of the Pharmakeute. That is to say, the memory of a people intimately and respectfully joined with the plant realm. The majority of the plants used by the Pharmakeute now constitute the classic list of the plants of Witchcraft. These particular plants were and are used to achieve altered states of consciousness, which is part of the Witch's power and path.

It seems clear that our ancestors believed in Otherworld communication, and that they felt guided and directed by what they perceived to be spirits, gods, and entities. In this way our ancestors came to obtain knowledge of mystical and hidden things. It is not an invention by an individual; it is a revealing to an individual from something outside. This revelation comes through an alignment that establishes communication with beings dwelling in nonmaterial reality.

The ancestral spirit speaks to us from the blood flowing through our veins, for it contains the memory of our lineage. There are other voices willing to inform us, and they whisper in the quiet times when we are receptive. We are connected to them when our spirits embrace the same things. A kindred connection forms when we emanate the love of the plant realm, when we sense the moon's light as sacred, and when we understand nature as self-aware. These are the stepping-stones that lead from the Witch's garden to the threshold of the Otherworld.

The Witch's garden contained plants with powerful properties to invoke altered states of consciousness. They were also capable of causing death, and it is from this nature that the term "poison path" is sometimes applied to Witchcraft. While it is true that such plants have a physical use in Witchcraft, there is also a parallel path—that of the spirit dancer, or what is known by practitioners as the backward dance. This involves inhaling the scent from the plant's blossoms; such an act serves to draw the plant spirit into the human body. This is a temporary type of possession, but it is actually a shared consciousness through which an intimate relationship is established. Through this act, a familiar-spirit bond is set in place. The backward dance is performed to turn symbolically from the material world into the spirit world. In accord, the dancer faces away from the tree or plant and circles three times around, always facing in the opposite direction.

In the practice of Old World Witchery, when physical plants are not available, plant spirit sigils can be used to evoke the entities. This practice is tied to essential occult tenets that are the foundation for opening portals between the worlds. Although having the material plant is preferred and subscribed, it is still possible to work as a Pharmakeute with only the sigils. It should also be noted that working solely with sigils is much safer than handling or ingesting poisonous plant material. Symbols of this nature can be found in my book *Grimoire of the Thorn-Blooded Witch*.

In modern times the goal is to win back the favor of the Greenwood realm through identification as a Pharmakeute. In the Ash, Birch and Willow tradition, this can be accomplished through a process that includes being bled by the pricking of a rose thorn. Three drops of blood are mixed with a cup of water, which is then poured upon the base of a rose bush. This act is performed in honor of She of the Thorn-Blooded Rose, and all who bare their flesh to her in this way come to be known as Thorn-Blooded Witches. This alignment bestows upon them the right to make the declaration of the Pharmakeute before performing any ritual, spell, or work of magic:

I am a Thorn-Blooded Witch of the Old Ways.

Roots beneath, hear me.

Shadow below, know me.

Branches above, connect me,

for in-between I stand

as a Thorn-Blooded Witch of the Old Ways.

In the words of the declaration, we find the initial and primal connections of the Witch with the land. As mentioned earlier in this chapter, this is the primal imprint of the ancestral forest experience. The declaration realigns the Pharmakeute to the branches that touch the realm above, to the roots that entwine the world of mortal kind, and to the memory that awaits deep within shadow. The Pharmakeute affirms that she or he is in the center of all, in the in-between place, which is the most magical place.

The Witch of the Greenwood is not limited to the material world but maintains her or his connection to the celestial. The Pharmakeute understands the relationship of light with the plant realm and the timing of the seasons. These relationships are written in the night sky by the moon and the stars and are led by the sun overhead. In the spiritual tradition of the Pharmakeute, the words of alignment help the Witch understand the purpose of the soul's place in, and journey through, her or his lifetime:

I am a Thorn-Blooded Witch of the Old Ways.

I am descended from the stars,

fated by the sun,

envisioned by the moon,

given form by the land,

and I stand with feet rooted in shadow,

and reach upwards towards the stars.

It is through the words of alignment that the memory of being spirit is retained in the body memory (so it does not become lost to sensory domination in the flesh). As the soul descends toward material incarnation, it is imprinted by the sun sign through which it enters physical birth. Fate is then the "blueprint" of the natal chart's nature upon the new personality, through which the soul will experience a given lifetime.

In occult philosophy, all material forms originate from an astral image, hence the idea of the soul being envisioned by the moon (a poetic sense of the process). Once the soul is coated with the etheric body, it is drawn by its now heavier density toward the material sphere. Here is it "given form by the land," meaning that the astral image passes with the encased soul into a material body. For the Pharmakeute, the memory of its origin amidst the stars, joined with access to the organic memory of the earth, maintains a higher consciousness. It is one not overpowered by the demands of material existence, which allows the soul to accomplish its purpose on earth while crafting its way back to the stars.

The aligned consciousness of the Pharmakeute allows the Witch to stretch forth her or his hands and call upon all that is connected. Here the Pharmakeute seeks to draw upon the stars and moon as well as the Spirit of the Land. The land links the Witch to the organic memory of the earth and the herbs of the plant realm that tap into it. All of these attachments join the Witch with the celestial and the terrestrial through nature and character, and so we enter into the occult axiom of "like attracts like."

Another occult axiom enters into the picture: "as above, so below." Just as a soul inhabits a flesh body, a spirit inhabits a plant body. In the spiritual tradition of the Pharmakeute, a plant spirit is a go-between that aids communication between the Witch and the Greenwood realm. However, beyond that, the plant spirit draws upon the organic memory of the earth under the direction of the Pharmakeute. Therefore, gaining a powerful plant spirit ally is crucial for the Greenwood Witch.

THE WITCH AND THE MANDRAKE

Folklorist H. F. Clark states that the mandrake once walked the earth as a goddess with the gift of love. He adds that the mandrake was also a frightful "fiend" that granted wealth, health, and fertility. Clark goes on to say that the price for these gifts was always death. He calls the mandrake the symbol of the apple of Aphrodite and recounts a tradition that involved dancing around the mandrake while talking of love matters the entire time.[6] Aphrodite was also known as *Mandragoritis*, or She of the Mandrake. As we will soon see in this section, the goddess of love plays an interesting role.

In the rich lore of the mandrake, we find the Witch, as a sorceress, embracing the Old Magic of the plant realm. The mandrake is the interface between plant kind and humankind. It is sometimes referred to as the plant that dreamed of being human, and therefore its roots took human form. Like humans, the mandrake could love, and it became valued for casting love spells. It is here that we encounter the goddess Venus, but not in the way most people might assume.

For centuries, Witchcraft was known as *venefica,* which replaced the earlier Greek word *pharmakis*. In Latin, the word originally used for Witch was *saga*, which indicates a fortune-teller or seer. This was later changed to *venefica*, a word that became linked to the use of poison. But as will shortly become clear, venefica has its earlier roots in the practice of preparing love potions.

The earliest laws against Witchcraft dealt with the use of herbal potions employed in love spells; the lawmakers believed that love spells "poisoned" the free will. However, the root word for *venefica* is the same as that for the word *venereal*, derived from the Latin *vene*, indicating a relationship to Venus. Another example of the benign *vene* root is *venerate*, which means "to regard with heartfelt deference." The etymology of the word *venom* connects with the Latin *venenum* (Vulgar Latin—*venimen*).

In his book *Phases in the Religion of Ancient Rome*, scholar Cyril Bailey mentions that Venus was originally a deity of gardens and vines, the cultivator. (This is also mentioned by scholar Albert Grenier in his book *The Roman Spirit.*) Putting this all together, we have Venus as a goddess of plants, and the Latin word *venefica* (replacing the Greek

---

6 H. F. Clark, "The Mandrake Fiend," *Folklore* 73, no. 4 (Winter 1962): 257–269.

pharmakis used to indicate one knowledgeable in plants), which suggests that early Witches were in some fashion associated with the goddess Venus, if only in their dealings with herbal love potions. There may well be more to this, however, for indeed many centuries later (1375 CE), a woman named Gabrina Albetti is convicted of practicing Witchcraft after confessing to going out at night, removing her clothing, and worshipping the brightest star in the sky. This bright light would actually have been the planet Venus, which shines brilliantly just before dawn as well as in the night sky. Add to this the old teaching that the pentagram symbolizes the star inside the full moon, and things become quite interesting.

The word *venefica* later evolved to indicate simply one who possessed knowledge of poisonous plants, and over the course of time this became its singular and specific meaning. The Roman historian Livy (first century CE) mentions the first trial for practicing veneficium having taken place in the early days of Rome.[7] Modern scholars assign the year 331 BCE to this trial. Reportedly, many mysterious deaths had occurred in the community, and no doubt the officials were hard-pressed by the citizens to explain what was going on.

Several women were rounded up and accused of making harmful potions, but the women claimed their potions were designed to heal. The officials produced a potion they claimed was made by the women and challenged them to drink it. The women agreed, but upon drinking the potion, they immediately died. The citizens were content that the problem was resolved. Whether the potions were actually made by the women or conveniently substituted with something lethal by the worried officials is another matter. Eventually, almost all Latin words for poison (venom) became attached

7 Liam Grandy, "Livy's Witch-hunts: A Study of Investigations into Veneficium Found in Livy" (master's thesis, Victoria University of Wellington, 2018), *https://researcharchive.vuw.ac.nz.*

to *vene* as a root word for poison, particularly when referring to Witches and Witchcraft. No doubt the Witch figure commanded respect but was also viewed with a healthy fear of his or her power and knowledge.

One popular mandrake legend makes the fear of this plant quite clear. The legend tells that whoever pulled a mandrake from the ground would die as a result. Therefore, a method was devised of tying a starving dog to a mandrake and then tossing food at a distance from the animal, causing the dog to lunge forward and uproot the mandrake. In this way, the human avoided death. A popular superstition connected to the mandrake is that it "screams" when it is pulled from the ground. In this lore its scream is said to be deadly. In the mystical tradition the lore is about the spirit entity within the plant who is driven out when the plant is assaulted in this way. The "scream" is the energy disturbance, which can be problematic for the person claiming the plant.

Mandrakes do not grow in abundance, and it may be that the frightening legends were actually invented with the intention of minimizing the harvesting of available plants. If so, did Witches initiate such legends to safeguard their supply, or did opponents of Witchcraft foster the tales to discourage people from wanting to use a mandrake for the purpose of magic? Whatever the truth may be, the mandrake still holds a dominant place in the history of the plants of Witchcraft.

In the practice of magic, the mandrake root is considered a powerful talisman. Its power is derived from the spirit inhabiting it. This spirit is connected with chthonic forces beneath the earth as well as with those who walk in the night. The mandrake spirit serves to link humankind with plant kind and is therefore a magical bridge to the Greenwood realm and the space of shadow from which all mysteries flow. In legend, the mandrake is known as the sorcerer's root and connects its possessor with the Old Magic. The mandrake spirit is evoked on a Monday at midnight with the Call of Enchantment:

You are the master at watch in the midnight hour,

The sorcerer's root of the Witch's power.

The plant who wanted human form,

Brings plant and Witch to covenants sworn.

Rooted dweller in the black earth unseen,

Hidden eyes peering to catch the moon's beam.

Leafy crown of stars, the Greenwood might,

Empowers the will through the Witch's rite.

Come to the Thorn-Blooded Witch who hails,

I call you to pass through the verdant veils.

I reach out from the time-honored power,

By seed, sprout, budded leaf, and flower.

The mandrake root talisman is carried in a black or red pouch concealed on the Witch's body. On the night of each full moon, the root is brought out and anointed with goat's milk, red wine, honey, and three drops of the Witch's blood. The root is then left in the moon's light and retrieved before the sun rises. Before returning the root to the pouch, the Witch thoroughly washes, cleans, and dries it. The Pharmakeute can then ask for the aid of the mandrake spirit for a specific desire to become manifest. All that remains is for the Witch to hold the mandrake root up to the moon and then present it to the west quarter. It may then be placed in its pouch.

MANDRAKE LORE

In old lore the Witch and the mandrake plant are almost inseparable. It is nearly impossible to think of plants associated with Witchcraft and not have the mandrake at or near the top of the list. It appears in ancient writings of the pre-Christian era and continues to be mentioned over the following centuries and into modern times. There are several plants given the name mandrake, although only two actually belong to the botanical group: *Mandragora officinalis* (or *officinarum*) and *Mandragora autumnalis*.

When the mandrake is mentioned in magical texts from Old England, the plant is actually the white bryony (*Bryonia dioica*); however, some commentators include the black bryony. The root and fruit of this English mandrake are similar to the "official" mandrake, which is native to southern Europe. The leaves of English mandrake, however, are very different and resemble some forms of ivy. The so-called American mandrake is commonly known as mayapple. Its botanical name is *Podophyllum peltatum*, and it is native to North America. The mayapple is toxic, and like the mandrake and the white bryony, it should be used with care.

The root of the mandrake is legendary and is often depicted in human form. Indeed, many mandrake roots are shaped like a human body and can grow up to three feet in length. They have a texture similar to a carrot but are thicker (sometimes as wide as a potato at the center of the root). Folkloric references sometimes call the mandrake "the plant that wanted to be human" or the "burrowed man" of the woods. However, not all mandrake roots resemble human form. In some cases the roots can be taken from the soil, carefully carved to look human, and placed back into the soil. The carved areas will heal and the root will continue to grow.

Old occult tales tell of the sorcerer's root and refer to it as "the master of all plants." This root is the mandrake and is traditionally carried in a pouch by the person who owns it. Each full moon, the root is anointed with scented oil (traditionally, Master Oil) and then left in the moonlight when the moon is directly overhead. It must be retrieved before sunrise.

In magical tradition, the mandrake root can be bathed in fresh water. The water is then put into a special bottle that is not used for anything else. It is said that if a person sprinkles this water on anything, it will flourish. This belief gave rise to the practice of sprinkling mandrake water on crop fields, herd animals, and money. In occult tradition, this boon is granted only once every four years, and therefore can only be performed in accordance with this cycle.

To carry a sorcerer's root is to be connected with the spirit of the mandrake species, the collective consciousness residing in the organic memory of the earth. The old belief is that the powers of the mandrake that lie beneath the earth can be invoked or evoked as desired. This ability increases the power of anyone who wields the sorcerer's root. In connection with this theme is the belief that the mandrake root grants influence over spirits of the dead; for this power the root must be anointed at a crossroads or in a cemetery on the dark moon.

The powerful nature of the mandrake is in sharp contrast to the fact that the plant itself is very sensitive. Too much water, too little water, digging the plant up, or even handling the leaves can cause the mandrake to sulk. In a short time it will lose its leaves and appear to be dead. One should not despair if a mandrake loses its leaves and new leaves do not appear for weeks or even months. The mandrake may simply be biding its time.

During the Christian era, the demonization of Pagan spirits and deities resulted in the depiction of the mandrake spirit as diabolical. The mandrake began to lose its mystical connection with the secret places in the woods where the magic users went to collect herbs. Gradually, the lore spoke of finding a mandrake beneath or near the place where a criminal was hung for his transgressions. Odd ideas formed around this new lore, and we find mention of the mandrake springing forth where the hanged man urinated upon the ground. This is an outgrowth of an earlier belief that the mandrake grows from semen spilled on the soil, and it takes on the form of a human as a result of this act.

In old Witch lore the mandrake is taken from the soil in a very special manner. The Witch faces west and traces three concentric circles around the plant. Returning to face west, he or she then pours a potion of milk and soothing herbs around the base of the mandrake. The Witch tells the plant why it is needed, asks permission to take a piece of root, and then removes the soil on one side of the mandrake, exposing its roots. Using a sharp knife, he or she quickly removes a piece of root and then returns the soil to fill the hole.

In some occult traditions the mandrake is called Circaeon, which identifies it with Circe, the powerful sorceress of ancient legend. In this regard, we can think of the mandrake as Circe's root (or plant). However, a long-standing tradition places the mandrake under the dominion of the goddess Hecate. She is often connected to the crossroads, a place in ancient beliefs where the dead gathered and where Witches came to practice their ways. As mentioned earlier, it was an ancient practice to erect a large wooden pole, called a hekataia or hekataeon, at the crossroads to represent the goddess Hecate. Another name for this pole was the tree of Hecate, which brings us full circle back to the connection with the forest, from which the Pharmakeute first came into spiritual-mindedness.

WOODLAND PRIESTS AND THE SABBATIC WAFER

Writings from the Middle Ages and Renaissance depict Witches gathering in secret places where they performed rites that seemingly contained elements of religion. Seventeenth-century Witch hunter Francesco Maria Guazzo, in his work *Compendium Maleficarum*, wrote that Witches read from a black book during their religious rites, and he notes a religious demeanor: "For witches observe various silences, measurings, vigils, mutterings, figures and fires, as if they were some expiatory religious rite."[8]

Guazzo goes on to describe the use of a stained black turnip as the "Elevation of the Host" at the Witch's Sabbat. And in Germany, turnip rinds and parings were reportedly served as the "Holy Eucharist."

One interesting element that appears on the folkloric level is that of the devil's turnip. The so-called English mandrake (*Bryonia dioica*), or white bryony, matches perfectly the description of the "sabbatic host" in appearance, odor, and taste, as found in writings about Witchcraft. It is one of several plants used by the Pharmakeute that has spiritual—some might say, religious—connotations tying it to the Otherworld and shamanic-like journeys.

The mandrake and other traditional plants in Witchcraft, such as belladonna, henbane, and monkshood, have their place in the Witch's Sabbat feast. One or more elements of a particular plant are added to the wine and bread, thereby aiding the mystical intention of the rite. In place of this, the inhaled spirit from the plant blossom can be passed on the breath into the wine and bread, or the two methods may be combined.

In one of the old legends about Witches, we find a special connection with the plant known as vervain. It appears on the old silver charm

---

8 Francesco Maria Guazzo, *Compendium Maleficarum*, trans. E. A. Ashwin (Mineola, NY: Dover Publications, 1988), 123.

known as the cimaruta (*chee-mah-roo-tah*), which is fashioned after a sprig of rue and bears various symbolic images. This is often called the Witch's charm and is believed by some to be worn as a sign of membership in the old society of Witches. Vervain is one of the faery plants, and is associated with the star Sirius. Its blossom has long been a sign of peace when carried by messengers, which connects it to the granting of safe passage (a theme found in the legendary silver bough tale).

On the cimaruta charm, the blossom represents the covenant between the Witch and the faery race. This is connected to the idea that Witches are the stewards of the Greenwood on the material realm and faeries are its stewards in the Otherworld. Here we find the concept of the two worlds (that of mortal kind and faery kind) along with the idea that they are connected through a passageway. In folkloric tales, the hollow of a tree is a doorway or portal into the faery realm.

The cimaruta charm strongly reflects the intimate connection between Witches and plants. We see reflections of this in the lore of Witches riding on branches, twigs, and brooms. Our ancestors believed that spirits inhabited trees and plants, and that the experience arising from ingesting plant material came from being possessed by its spirit. It is in this enchanted worldview that we find the spiritual tradition of the Pharmakeute.

Writings about the ritual meal of the Sabbat contain references to sacred or magical wafers (or bread). One example can be found in Leland's *Aradia*. The author includes a chapter titled "The Sabbat—Treguenda or Witch-Meeting," which outlines how to consecrate the supper.[9] The meal consists of cakes made from grain, wine, salt, and honey that are shaped into crescent moons. There are other references to this meal from a different area of Europe and the British Isles. While these references differ in several ways from the meal described

---

9 Charles Godfrey Leland, *Aradia: Or the Gospel of the Witches* (London: David Nutt, 1899), xiii.

in Leland's writings, they still connect with plants through the plant material in the form of wafers.

Some commentators on Witchcraft depict the Sabbat as a parody of the Catholic mass in which the holy communion wafer is abused. These alleged practices can be found in the following passages:

> *The hosts are then brought to the altar. Boguet describes them as dark and round, stamped with a hideous design; Madeleine Bavent saw them as ordinary wafers only coloured red; in other cases they were black and triangular in shape.*[10]

> *But there is talk of anointing a stick, and of wafers stamped with the Devil's name, and of an attendant imp by the name of Robert Artisson . . .*[11]

> *It was an era of Black Masses . . . persons were accused of such sacrilegious acts as using communion wafers for sodomistic purposes . . .*[12]

> *Clement scornfully revealed what was in the "mystic chests" of the mysteries: ". . . sesame cakes, and pyramidal cakes, and globular and flat cakes, embossed with lumps of salt, and with a serpent, the symbol of Dionysus Bassareus. . . ." In Rome such cakes are mentioned especially in connection with Priapus, a god of fertility, who was represented by an oversized phallus.*[13]

---

10 Montague Summers, *History of Witchcraft and Demonology* (Whitefish, MT: Kessinger, 2003), 155.

11 Elliot Rose, *A Razor for a Goat: Problems in the History of Witchcraft and Diabolism* (Toronto, ON: University of Toronto Press, 1989), 66.

12 Armando R. Favazza, *Bodies Under Siege: Self-Mutilation and Body Modification in Culture and Psychiatry* (Baltimore, MD: Johns Hopkins University Press, 1996), 10.

13 Stephen Benko, *The Virgin Goddess: Studies in the Pagan and Christian Roots of Mariology* (Leiden, Netherlands: Brill, 2003), 179.

Then came another swinish farce, described by Lancre and Boguet, in which some young and pretty wife would take the Witch's place as Queen of the Sabbath, and submit her body to the vilest handling. A farce not less repulsive was the "Black Sacrament," performed with a black radish, which Satan would cut into little pieces and gravely swallow.[14]

Hiding in these passages are elements of an older non-Christian theme, which Leland touched on briefly. In *Aradia*, he provides the conjuration of the Sabbat meal:

I conjure thee, O Meal!

Who art indeed our body, since without thee

We could not live, thou who (at first as seed)

Before becoming flower went in the earth,

Where all deep secrets hide, and then when ground

Didst dance like dust in the wind, and yet meanwhile

Didst bear with thee in flitting, secrets strange!

And yet erewhile, when thou wert in the ear,

Even as a (golden) glittering grain, even then

The fireflies came to cast on thee their light

And aid thy growth, because without their help

Thou couldst not grow nor beautiful become;

Therefore thou dost belong unto the race

---

14 Jules Michelet, *La Sorcière: The Witch of the Middle Ages*, trans. L. J. Trotter (London: Simpkin, Marshall, and Co., 1863), 221.

Of witches or of fairies, and because

The fireflies do belong unto the sun. . . .

Queen of the Fireflies! hurry apace,

Come to me now as if running a race,

Bridle the horse as you hear me now sing!

Bridle, O bridle the son of the king!

Come in a hurry and bring him to me!

The son of the king will ere long set thee free;

And because thou for ever art brilliant and fair,

Under a glass I will keep thee; while there,

With a lens I will study thy secrets concealed,

Till all their bright mysteries are fully revealed,

Yea, all the wondrous lore perplexed

Of this life of our cross and of the next.

Thus to all mysteries I shall attain,

Yea, even to that at last of the grain;

And when this at last I shall truly know,

Firefly, freely I'll let thee go!

When Earth's dark secrets are known to me,

My blessing at last I will give to thee![15]

---

15 Leland, *Aradia,* 10–11.

From an occult perspective, these verses speak to elements of the Agricultural Mysteries, and tie well into the Sabbat meal as a spiritual tradition. The seed can be thought of as absorbing the Chthonic Mysteries as it rests in the darkness beneath the earth. Then, when it pushes up and into the world of light, it receives the celestial counterpart of the Inner Mysteries. In old Italian lore, this is illustrated by the appearance of fireflies (also known as lightning bugs). In Italy they are called *lucciola,* and in days of old they were thought to be faeries. On the summer solstice, just after dusk, swarms of fireflies descend upon the wheat fields and land on the tips of the grain stalks. This gave the appearance of faeries amidst the planted field.

In the mystical tradition, wheat spikes hold the mysteries of the Underworld, which were drawn up by the roots of the plants. The *lucciola*, as a faery spirit, lands on the tips of the wheat spike and imparts the mysteries of the star realm. Later the wheat will be used to make ritual bread that is used in a type of communion meal through which the Inner Mysteries are taken into the bodies, minds, and spirits of the participants. The words of communion illustrate the mystical process:

> *"Blessings upon this meal, which is as our own body. For without this, we ourselves would perish from this world. Blessings upon the grain, which as seed went into the earth, where deep secrets hide. And there did dance with the elements, and spring forth as flowered plant, concealing secrets strange. When you were in the ear of grain, spirits of the field came to cast their light upon you, and aid you in your growth. Thus through you we shall be touched by that same race, and the mysteries hidden within you we shall obtain even unto the last of these grains."*

The Grain Mysteries are associated with a spirit called Lucifero, who, in his chthonic guise, is known as Noctifer or Nottambulo (the night walker). This spirit is also known as Lucifer, the light-herald or light-bearer. The light of the stars in the Underworld, emanating from Lucifer, gives illumination in every sense of the word. It is the mystery teaching that light is at home in the darkness—literally, enlightenment in the places of darkness.

The mythos of Lucifero depicts him as a star-being who descended to earth with such velocity that he penetrated deep into the land. In his former realm he was known as star seeder, the light of renewal, just as Lucibello is the renewer of light at the mating of fireflies in the wheat fields on the summer solstice. Lucifero offers light and enlightenment wherever it is absent, and he is the revealer of the hidden mysteries. It is through his descent to earth, and his penetration into the dark realm below, that Lucifero impregnates the earth with revealing light. The falling stars that connect with his mythos are sometimes regarded as his allies or fellow star-beings who join him on earth.

In this mythos, we can envision the Witch as a type of priestess or priest of the Old Ways that connects the night sky with the deep places of the earth, a kinship of fire and light, above and below. In this role the Witch directs and partakes of the Sabbat meal. The wine, made from plants, represents the formless from which form can arise. In this sense, it is the celestial wholeness, the black night sky made liquid. The bread or wafer, made from grain, represents the formation of the Mysteries (above and below) that can be placed into the hands of the Witch. Once ingested, the Sabbat meal transforms the mind, body, and spirit of the Witch. This is the sacred transformation of the Greenwood magic that holds the mystical waft in the branches of trees beneath the full moon.

Night is always the sacred time in Witchcraft. Invocations spoken beneath the moon and stars are timeless. One ancient example appears in Ovid's *Metamorphoses*. The evocations used by the Witch Medea, in the tales about her, are remarkably similar to even more ancient evocations of historical record, such as those from Babylonia addressed to the Lady of the Silence of the Night, the Night Bride, or the Veiled Bride. The evocation in Ovid's work has Medea calling upon the night-wandering queen, who looks kindly upon this undertaking.[16]

In these verses, we catch a glimpse of some very primal elements of Witchcraft such as drawing upon the things and forces of nature. It is from this foundation that we encounter the Witch as Pharmakeute, one who intimately knows the Spirit of the Land. The consciousness of the land is intimately linked to the vegetation, and particularly to trees. In the midst of a grove stands the one sacred tree that is the voice of the spirit of the place. It is the spiritual center for the Witch, the woodland temple of the Greenwood realm.

THE ANCIENT MAGIC

Witchcraft in ancient times is depicted as exclusively assigned to women. In ancient Greece it was referred to as an illicit religion as well as a feared system of magic. The history of Witchcraft includes not only charges of magic but also combines prostitution and banned acts of sexuality. At the core of such laws and prohibitions is a deep-rooted male fear of female sexuality and its alluring power over men.

Among the earliest appearances of a Witch in ancient writings again we find the figure known as Medea. In the tales associated with Jason and the Argonauts, Medea is depicted as harvesting herbs with her dress undone and open. In other writings she is depicted as being seminude. The ancient Witch known as Pamphile is portrayed as practicing completely naked. The ancient writer Apuleius

---

16 Ovid, *Metamorphoses*, trans. David Raeburn (New York: Penguin Books, 2004).

(*Metamorphoses* 3.15–25) describes her as a Thessalian Witch who removes all of her clothing and smears her body with ointment.

Nudity continues to be associated with Witches well into the Christian era. Historian Jeffrey Burton Russell writes, "A woman named Marta was tortured in Florence about 1375: she was alleged to have placed candles round a dish and to have taken off her clothes and stood above the dish in the nude, making magical signs."[17]

Historian Ruth Martin, in her book *Witchcraft and the Inquisition in Venice 1550–1650*, comments that it was a common practice for Witches of this era to be "naked with their hair loose around their shoulders" while reciting conjurations.[18] In addition, there are several examples of nudity appearing in various seventeenth-century woodcuts that depict Witches dancing naked.

One dominating feature of ancient Witchcraft is the ritual and magical cauldron. The cauldron has long been associated with women and feminine symbolism in general. Scholar Erich Neumann, in his classic work *The Great Mother*, wrote:

> *[T]his transformation, which is viewed as magical, can only be effected by the woman because she herself, in her body that corresponds to the Great Goddess, is the cauldron of incarnation, birth and rebirth. And that is why the magical cauldron or pot is always in the hand of the female mana figure, the priestess or, later, the witch.*[19]

In the ancient tales of Medea, the cauldron is depicted as a vessel of transformation. As such it can renew life and vitality as well as draw

---

17 Jeffrey Burton Russell, *Witchcraft in the Middles Ages* (Ithaca, New York: Cornell University Press, 1984), 210.

18 Ruth Martin, *Witchcraft and the Inquisition in Venice, 1550–1650* (New York: Basil Blackwell, 1989).

19 Erich Neumann, *The Great Mother: An Analysis of the Archetype,* trans. Ralph Manheim (Princeton, NJ: Princeton University Press, 2015), 287–288.

it back into its depths. In many regions of Europe, we find tales of the cauldron associated with such goddess figures as Ceres and Cerridwen. In ancient tales the cauldron often appears hidden in a cave, a dungeon, or the Underworld. This speaks of its secret or hidden nature, and of its connection with the Otherworld. As a tool associated with life and death, the cauldron is intimately connected to souls of the dead. This is one of the reasons why the skull often appears with the cauldron (as well as bones in general).

In ancient times the cauldron was suspended within the hearth. The hearth is the symbol of the sacred grotto where the goddess was originally worshipped. The stones of the hearth represent this ancient setting. The opening of the hearth symbolizes the cave, the ancient entrance into the Underworld. The fire burning within the hearth is the divine flame, the oldest representation of the goddess in her purity without human form. This is one of the reasons why the goddesses of Witchcraft carry lighted torches. The other reason is that goddesses of the torch-bearing classification are connected to the moon, and torches represent light in the darkness.

Fire, as a representation of the goddess in her primal nature, symbolizes her as unclothed and liberated. The flicker of torchlight on the nude bodies of Witches conveys the liberating power of the goddess to her followers. This meaning is reflected in the text known as the Charge of Aradia used in the Italian Witchcraft tradition I taught:

> *Whenever you have need of anything, once in the month when the moon is full, then shall you come together at some deserted place, or where there are woods, and give worship to She who is Queen of all Witches.*
>
> *Come all together inside a circle, and secrets that are as yet unknown shall be revealed. And your mind must be free and*

also your spirit, and as a sign that you are truly free, you shall be naked in your rites. And you shall rejoice and sing, making music and love. For this is the essence of spirit, and the knowledge of joy.

Be true to your own beliefs, and keep to the ways, beyond all obstacles. For ours is the key to the mysteries and the cycle of rebirth, which opens the way to the Womb of Enlightenment. I am the spirit of Witches all, and this is joy and peace and harmony.[20]

DRAWING DOWN THE MOON

Ancient pre-Christian writings of Greece and Rome depict Witches performing acts of magic associated with the moon. One dominant theme portrays Witches as being able to draw the moon down from the sky. Various ancient authors held differing views as to what this meant.

Historian Daniel Ogden points out in his book *Magic, Witchcraft, and Ghosts in the Greek and Roman Worlds* that the act of drawing down the moon incorporated erotic attraction magic. This is another reason for ritual nudity. The long-standing tradition of the moon as a fertile agent, and romance connected to the full moon, are remnants of this ancient tradition.

In the ancient text of the *Metamorphoses* (of Apuleius) we find the idea that drawing down the moon leaves a deposit of foam on the ground, which is called the virus lunare, or moon juice. This substance is used for magical purposes. Unknown to the ancient scholars, the substance was actually the morning dew left on lichen that grows on rocks. This is captured in a chant of Old Witchery:

---

20 Raven Grimassi, *Hereditary Witchcraft: Secrets of the Old Religion* (St. Paul, MN: Llewellyn, 1999), 131.

"What we knew in the night

'neath the moon full and bright,

wakes the stone and the bone,

and then come we who gather the loam."

The lichen was grayish-white, and the spots of it on the rocks looked much like the patterns one sees with the naked eye when looking at the surface of the full moon.

According to oral tradition, the heavy dew following the night of a full moon was collected on leaves and then poured into a small container. The dew was then used in magical spells and for blessings, healings, and anointing.

The connection of the moon to water is also noted in the teachings regarding the moon's reflection on the surface of lakes and oceans. At Lake Nemi, Italy, where the temple of Diana once stood, the lake was known as Diana's Mirror. This was because of the full moon's reflection on the surface of the calm lake, which could be easily seen from the temple itself. It is noteworthy that Diana was known in ancient times also by the epithet of "the Dewy One."

The Roman poet Horace writes in the *Epodes* that witches use a book by which they can call down the moon with incantations. He also depicts Witches calling upon Diana to aid them in their night dealings. Horace refers to a Witch's book known as the *libro carminun*, which means the book of songs, or the book of enchantment. In Epode 5, we find these Latin words spoken by the Witch known as Canidia:

Nox et Diana, quae silentium regis,

arcana cum fiunt sacra,

nunc, nunc adeste, nunc in hostilis domos

iram atque numen uertite.[21]

Here's my translation:

Night and Diana, who command silence

when secret mysteries are performed;

now, now aid me: now turn your vengeance and influence

against my enemies' houses.

It is noteworthy that in the writings of Charles Leland we also find this theme related to Italian Witchcraft. Leland portrays Aradia (in the personage of the daughter of Diana) as a Witch who fights against the oppression of peasants by the noble class. This theme is also found in the words of the closing prayer in the full moon ritual:

"Give us power, O' Most Secret Lady, to bind our oppressors. Receive us as Your children, receive us though we are earthbound. When our bodies lie resting nightly, speak to our inner spirits, teach us all Your Holy Mysteries. I believe Your ancient promise that we who seek Your Holy Presence will receive of Your wisdom."

In this text we also find the idea of a covenant between the Witch and her or his deity. At the core is a promise, and therefore a trust of that promise.

In the following ancient incantation there appears a mention of the night as the keeper of secrets. There is also mention of the stars and the moon bearing witness to the deeds of the Witch. We encountered this passage earlier, but it's repeated here for a new context:

---

21 Horace, *Epodes,* ed. David Mankin (New York: Cambridge University Press, 1995), 33.

"Night, trustiest keeper of my secrets, and stars who, together with the moon, follow on from the fires of the daylight,

And you, Hecate of the three heads, who know all about my designs and come to help the incantations and the craft of the witches,

And Earth, who furnishes witches with powerful herbs, and breezes, winds, mountains, rivers, and lakes, and all the gods of the groves and all the gods of the night, be present to help me.

Night-wandering queen, look kindly upon this undertaking."

The observation or witnessing of these rites is a very old theme. Remnants of it appear in archaic Roman religion (itself derived from Etruscan religion). We know from ancient sources that Witches gathered at the crossroads to perform their rituals and magic. In early Roman religion the crossroads was also the place where veneration of the ancestral lare spirits took place. Ovid, in *Fausti*, calls the lare the night watchmen. Scholar Georges Dumézil states that the lare were associated with points of demarcation areas and towers, as well as the agricultural seasons.[22]

This ancient theme appears to be reflected in the modern Wiccan concept of the Watchers and the watchtowers. However, in Old Witchery the Watchers are associated with the stars. Therefore, they possess a celestial nature as opposed to the terrestrial nature of the lare. The latter are also associated with bloodlines, and in this way they mark a lineage.

---

22 Georges Dumézil, *Archaic Roman Religion*, vol. 1, trans. Philip Krapp (Baltimore, MD: Johns Hopkins University Press, 1996), 340–346.

WITCHCRAFT AT THE CROSSROADS

Since ancient times the crossroads have been intimately linked to Witches, Witchcraft, and the goddess Hecate. As previously noted, Hecate is one of the oldest goddesses associated with Witchcraft. We also noted that it was the custom in ancient times to erect a hekataeon, a tree trunk, at the center of the crossroads, which represented her triple nature.

Hecate is often equated with Enodia, a Greek goddess whose name means "in-the-road" and who guarded entrances. The key was a cult symbol among Enodia's worshippers, as well as Hecate's. In ancient times the threshold of a doorway or gateway was a liminal area, which means a place in-between. This was also true of the crossroads, for the place where the roads came together was "in-between" the paths.

It was an ancient belief that souls who passed from life through a tragic, unjust, or violent death found it difficult to cross over into the Otherworld. These lost souls were believed to gather at the crossroads, a place between the worlds, awaiting Hecate's protection and guidance. One of the legends attached to Hecate portrays her leading this band of lost souls in night processions. This may well be the origin of the Church's Canon *Episcopi*, which warns against the belief that some women travel with the goddess Diana across great distances at night. Here is an excerpt:

> *Some wicked women are perverted by the Devil and led astray by illusions and fantasies induced by Daemons, so that they believe that they ride out at night with Diana the pagan Goddess . . . to a meeting to commune and do Her will flying across great distances. . . . Many other people also believe this to be true although it is a pagan error to believe that any other divinity exists than the one true God. . . . He [Satan] shows her deluded mind strange things and*

leads it on weird journeys. It is only the mind that does this. But faithless people believe that these things happen to the body as well.[23]

This text appears to be an attempt to discredit Pagan beliefs and practices, while at the same time bringing in the Christian devil figure to further distort and discourage adherence to the Old Religion.

We know from ancient sources that Roman Witches favored the crossroads for their night rituals and works of magic. A skull was placed there, along with two crossbones, to call in the ancestral spirits. Pomegranates, when in season, were special offerings to Hecate and to the spirits gathered at the crossroads. Offerings of coins, grain, and wine were given to the chthonic deities. Spelt "cakes" were tossed up into the night sky as an offering to the entities of the night, the stars, and the moon. Here again we see the ongoing importance of continuously uniting the celestial with the terrestrial.

In Old Witchery, for works of magic, a large Y was etched into the soil with a beech wand, and in the crux of the Y a symbol was placed to indicate the desired intent of the spell. The Y symbolizes the female power, as it represents the female genitalia (and therefore the vessel of generation). As the spell was recited, a circle was etched around the shape with the handle of a broom (clockwise) to enclose it as the power was being raised or drawn. Once fully formulated, the spell was released by sweeping the circle away with a broom (counterclockwise). The broom was then lifted upward and swung around to "fling" the power off toward the direction of the target of the spell.

The practice of ancestral veneration is noted in the use of poppets at the crossroads. Witches danced at the crossroads with their ancestors by tossing the poppets back and forth in merriment while

---

23 Jeffrey Burton Russell, *A History of Witchcraft: Sorcerers, Heretics, and Pagans* (London: Thames and Hudson, 1980), 53–54.

dancing and singing. Following the dance, the poppets where placed in the cauldron to aid the rebirth of the ancestral souls. It may be the case that this act, when viewed by spies from a distance at night, made onlookers believe that the Witches were putting babies in the cauldron. By flickering torchlight, the limp poppets may have looked like dead infants.

To invoke the ancestors, the Witches pricked themselves and offered drops of their blood. This was done in the belief that the dead required blood in order to animate in the world of the living. Therefore, the blood gave them vitality when they were drawn to the Witches' rituals. Feasting was also part of the ritual, and places were set for the dead to partake of the festivities.

The assemblies of Witches were all under the auspices of Hecate. Her hekataeon was the sacred tree of the worlds, which touched the realms beneath the earth and above it, as well as dwelling within the mortal realm itself. Around the tree the Witches danced beneath the full moon, joining with the spirits of those who danced before them in the distant past. It was at the crossroads where magic poured in from the Otherworld, pooled, and then poured back to its source.

THE MAGIC OF MOONLIGHT

An ancient belief held that the light of the full moon possessed magical properties. This appears in old folk beliefs about moonlight falling upon the crops to make them fertile. A related belief was that if a woman slept nude in a field beneath the full moon and awoke covered with the morning dew she would be made fertile. During the Christian era the Church sought to instill negative views about the moon. This is the era in which we find writings that if the moonlight falls upon a person while he or she is asleep, then insanity may occur. This is also the period of writings on the full moon turning people into werewolves.

We know from ancient sources that the light of the full moon was considered to be both sacred and magical. As mentioned previously, the reflection of the moon on Lake Nemi was viewed as the face of the goddess Diana. In magical and ritual practices, mirrors were used to reflect the moon's light for certain intentions. These mirrors were made of polished silver, bronze, or copper. One technique involved reflecting the light of the full moon onto the forehead of a priestess. She stood with the moon behind her, and the assistant knelt and angled the mirror to reflect the light. A series of mirrors was also used to reflect light into a bowl or box. It was believed that the magical essence of the moon's light could be captured and stored in this way. This allowed access to the powers inherent in the full moon at any time of the month.

The light of the full moon was used to magically charge rings, talismans, amulets, potions, and ritual tools. This could be performed by "snatching" the moon's light, which involved using the left hand like a bird's talons, while looking at the moon with the right eye closed. The moonlight was captured in the talons with a circular sweeping motion of the hand, and then the light of the moon was dragged downward and directed into the object to be charged. This required releasing the light by opening the fingers and pressing down on the object with the fingertips.

A tradition grew around this practice, which then associated the placement of the moon in one of the zodiac signs. This was believed to enhance the moon's power at such a time. The following are the traditional assigned occult influences when the moon passes into a particular zodiac sign:

- Moon in Aries: amplifies forces, brings additional power
- Moon in Taurus: draws personal favor from others
- Moon in Gemini: enhances receptivity in any matter

- Moon in Cancer: stirs the subconscious, influences dreams
- Moon in Leo: influences and enhances one's social position
- Moon in Virgo: brings focus and organization (attention to detail)
- Moon in Libra: stabilizes partnerships and relationships
- Moon in Scorpio: cloaks, maintains secrecy, keeps things unrevealed or obscure
- Moon in Sagittarius: brings about reform and change
- Moon in Capricorn: enhances logic and reason
- Moon in Aquarius: influences change and enhances projected image
- Moon in Pisces: enhances psychic energy and stimulates the emotions

CHAPTER THREE

THE MANY WORLDS

"O, let not the flame die out! Cherished age after age in its dark cavern—in its holy temples cherished. Fed by pure ministers of love—let not the flame die out!"

—THREE INITIATES, *THE KYBALION*

A key metaphysical principle exists in the axiom "as above, so below." This refers to the concept that the material plane is tied to the celestial (or divine) plane, and that the higher plane is reflected in the lower plane. However, because of the density of the material realm, the vision of the higher plane is not as obvious. We can liken this to looking at a car engine but not fully understanding the unseen process that makes it operational.

At the core of the axiom we can see the interlaced principle, and from this we note that the higher plane guides the lower plane. Through this there is communication; however, it goes both ways. On the earth plane we have "cause and effect," which can be seen as originating in the higher plane; but it can also be seen as the action here affecting the energy in the higher planes. This would cause a reaction, which in turn would create a transmission from the higher to the lower plane. Here again we find ourselves in the "as above, so below" scenario, but viewed in reverse. It is important to understand that the higher always "wins out," so to speak.

Many people credit the mystical writings of the legendary Hermes Trismegistus as the origin of this principle, which later entered

Witchcraft. His writings appear in what is called the Emerald Tablet, where we find these passages:

> *1. I speak not fictitious things, but what is true and most certain.*
>
> *2. What is below is like that which is above, and what is above is similar to that which is below, to accomplish the miracles of one thing.*
>
> *3. And as all things were produced by the mediation of one Being, so all things were formed from this one thing by adaptation.*
>
> *4. Its father is Sol, its mother Luna, the earth is its nurse.*
>
> *5. It is the cause of all perfection throughout the whole world.*
>
> *6. The power is perfect, if it be changed into earth.*
>
> *7. Separate the earth from the fire, the subtile from the gross, acting prudently and with judgment.*
>
> *8. Ascend with the greatest sagacity from the earth to heaven, and then again descend to the earth, and unite together the power of things superior and things inferior. Thus you will possess the glory of the whole world, and all obscurity will fly far away from you.*
>
> *9. This thing has more fortitude than fortitude itself, because it will overcome every subtile thing and penetrate every solid thing.*
>
> *10. By it this world was formed.*[1]

---

1 John C. Draper, "Alchemy and Chemistry," in *The American Chemist* V, no. 1. July 1874, 2. *www.google.com/books.*

In this principle we find that humankind is the microcosm of the universe. Theosophic occultism teaches that no form can be given to anything, either by nature or by man, whose ideal type does not already exist on the subjective plane. More than this, no such form or shape can possibly enter man's consciousness, or evolve in his imagination, which does not exist in prototype. It is taught that what takes place on the spiritual plane repeats itself on the cosmic plane. Concretion follows the lines of abstraction; corresponding to the highest must be the lowest, the material to the spiritual.

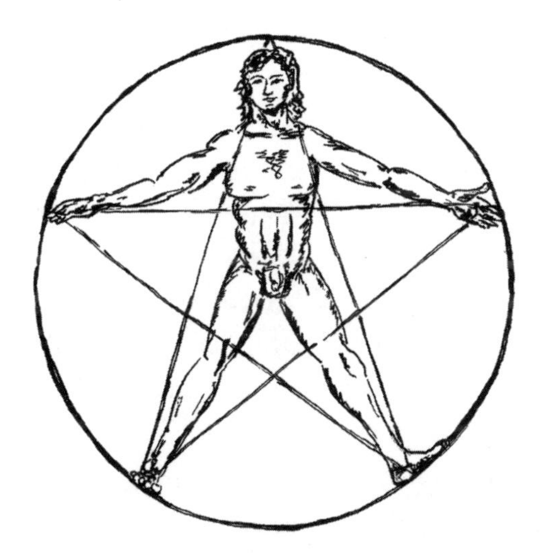

What all of this is telling us is that the universe is flowing into us as its counterpart on a microcosmic level. It is informing us just as it is drawing information from us. Our experience within its creation is examined by the universe (that is, the divine consciousness) and is used to adjust and modify reality over the course of the ages.

In this principle we find an inner mechanism. This is the core of universal activity, and it is all about balance. The universe restores balance. It counters chaos. Sometimes this calls for turmoil, conflict, protests, revolutions, and even war. From the ashes arise the new order of things. This is because we are the agents of change in the material creation of the universe, except that in our case it is currently a planetary arena. However, the stars are watching and taking note.

BETWEEN THE WORLDS

Among the foundational teachings is the concept of "between the worlds." The idea is that a magical corridor exists that separates material reality from nonmaterial reality. The two do not touch each other.

It is in the casting of a circle that the Witch enters the zone that is between the worlds. This zone is not inside the circle and also not in the dimension on the other side of nonmaterial reality. The benefit of this occult zone is that it is not subject to the limiting constraints of the material dimension. It is also not subject to the shifting formlessness (or fluidity) of nonmaterial reality. This condition allows the Witch to freely create the magical vessel that will contain the embedded imprint representing the magical desire or ritual intent. Here the Witch can freely create images or sigils that are limited only by the imagination.

In the Rooted Ways casting a circle forms around the mystical idea of joining together the moon and a mystical star. This is tied to an old Witch legend about the star and the crescent moon. When the waxing crescent moon is seen with a bright star next to it, the story goes that the moon is impregnated by the star. In this light the five-pointed star inside a circle represents the moon being pregnant with the star-child. This later appears in Witch lore as the herald of light and banisher of darkness.

In casting a ritual circle area on the ground, the Witch's blade is raised up to the stars. The tip of the blade is envisioned as hooking the brightest star (typically the planet Venus) and pulling it down to earth. Using the blade, a five-pointed star is traced in the air over each of the quarter directions: east, south, west, and north. Once completed, a five-pointed star is evoked on the ground within the closed circle. Viewed from above, it would appear as a pentagram.

In the Rooted Ways the circle is one circle within another. They are close together and form a corridor; it is a zone that is not inside or outside the ritual area. The ritualist parts the interior edge of the circle to open a way into the outer circle. All gestures and ritual calls are performed in the corridor facing the appropriate quarter. One example is evoking the Watchers or elementals. This includes calling the quarters, as it is known in contemporary Witchcraft.

THE WITCH'S CIRCLE

The magical idea of the circle in the Arts of Witchcraft is intimately linked to the number of the moon in occult correspondence. Here we find the number nine, which represents completion. Nine contains the actualization of all the possibilities. It possesses three sets of three, each of which is a triangle of manifestation containing the circulation of all the principles of reality.

The magical principle of nine allows for the view that all things within the circle return to itself. This "self-completion" is a reflection of the nature of the Divine Source of All Things in as much as the circle is the mirror image (the "as above, so below") of the mechanism.

The Witch's circle bears a five-pointed star traced upon the ground, which is enclosed in a circle. This gives us the number five. To this we add the four quarters of the circle, which gives us nine. This is the resonance of the Witch's circle.

The energy of nine circulates all things in itself. Casting the circle is an "artificial" means of attempting to conceive what is actually boundless and infinite within the Divine Source. The circle involves us in laying out a boundary without limiting the higher view. In this way we can grasp the temporary need of the concept that infinity is not unbounded or unordered when we encounter it. From a mystical perspective, nine adds a circumference to the circle that is nowhere and yet whose center is everywhere. In this way the circle bends back upon itself, thus granting us our differing concept of infinity for the purposes of working within a circle structure.

The five-pointed star holds the key to placing boundary within the boundless. The idea of the Witch and the star is timeless. Something of its magic is retained in the relatively modern depiction of the magical imagery of a wand mounted with a star.

In chapter 1 we noted the importance of the star pentacle that joins the chthonic and celestial realms. Here we found the so-called morning star and evening star. In the pentacle symbolism the star is embedded within the moon. The Witch lays out the star within the ritual circle. In this "as above, so below" action the circle is woven with a web of starlight in the form of an interlaced star.

The interlaced star holds the circle intact and enables it to maintain its energy field during the ritual or magical work. The star, because of its dual nature (as above, so below), readily opens the corridor between the worlds. This is the "lane" that appears inside the rim of the two concentric circles.

There is a noteworthy connection between the Witch's star and what is known as the Star Lantern. The latter is part of the faery realm legend. It is found most cohesive in the Ash, Birch and Willow tradition of Old Witchery. The tale is about the faery race known as the Lantra who are the Keepers of the Blue Flame, which is also called Starfire.

Starfire is the presence of the fifth element, which is aether, or spirit. It dispels the darkness, and in its presence no evil being, or being of ill intent, may remain. In this light the Lantra protect the material dimension from the unwanted presence and influence of evil beings. It's not their sole purpose, but it is part of their soul service.

One thing to bear in mind is that the five-pointed star is the design of the inner activity of the quintessence. It is within the Witch and also outside of the Witch. Earlier we encountered the image of "man" set within the pentacle. This is a reminder of what the Witch carries with her or him. The Witch is the true star wielder.

THE ASTRAL DIMENSION

In metaphysics the astral plane is a realm in which anything imagined can manifest in the material realm. From this principle arises that axiom that "thoughts are things." One example is this book you are reading. It is the manifestation of my thoughts that are now embedded in a material form (or in the case of electronics, they are accessible through a material device). But prior to writing the book, where did my thoughts come from? How did they manifest? It required a process within a nonmaterial realm.

I think of the astral plane as being composed of a liquid, plastic-like material, an etheric substance that forms around anything entering the astral dimension. One example I frequently use is to compare it to large bowl of melted wax. If you place your hand in the melted wax, it forms around it and creates a wax replica. The wax has changed from liquid to solid. This is what happens when a cohesive thought enters the astral dimension.

When the natural liquid state of the astral plane changes to something solid, that object is no longer compatible to the astral nature. Therefore, it cannot remain in the dimension. As a result, the object moves toward what it is compatible with, which is the material plane. This is how thoughts become things.

It is important to note that not all thoughts become things. The thought must be cohesive and strong, and it must be directed into the astral substance. This is covered in chapter 5. A flighty thought, as in daydreaming, is not cohesive; it is wishful. A formed thought, on the other hand, is another and different matter. It must be intentionally shaped and empowered. This requires full attention, focus, and concentration. Once this is coated in the astral substance, it is carried off by the plane of forces, which is more popularly known as the elemental plane.

THE ELEMENTAL PLANE

In metaphysics the elemental plane is the home of the creative elements of air, fire, water, and earth. It sits between the material and the astral plane with access to both dimensions. We can envision the elemental plane like a circular river flowing through the material and astral realms. The current carries things to and from each dimension. In this way thoughts are sent from the material realm into the astral, and formed thoughts are carried back to the material reality.

In ritual use the elemental plane provides access to the building blocks of creation. Each element of air, fire, water, and earth brings a magical nature to the setting and work at hand. Air provides transmission, which is the sending and receiving force. In the case of casting a circle, transmission communicates the intention. Fire brings the force of manifestation, which changes the mundane into the magical. In this way a circle marked upon the ground becomes a force field. Water ushers in the force of movement or flow. This element keeps the ritual circle vitalized, much like blood pumping through the body. Earth provides cohesion. In this way the circle becomes real in the material sense and holds all the elemental forces in place.

Traditionally, the elements are evoked at particular quarter markers around the circle. Air is evoked at the east quarter where the moon rises, and provides transmission of thought. Fire is evoked at the south quarter, where astral forces originate, and provides transformation of energy. Water is evoked at the west quarter, where tide and flow usher in, and provides movement, direction, and cleansing. Earth is evoked at the north quarter, where the power of the land resonates, and provides stability and cohesion.

In the casting of a ritual circle, or the creation of sacred space, the elements lend their nature to the setting. With the elemental energy present, the circle is attached to both worlds (material and elemental). This allows the energy raised within it to be directed out into other dimensions. The first realm is the elemental, which in turn passes the energy to the astral realm.

THE VOICE OF THE WIND

In the Rooted Ways we find the concept of the voice of the wind, which was very popular back in the 1960s. In part it refers to being taught by spirits, and in part it also refers to personal intuition. To hear the voice of the wind, in a metaphorical sense, means to be the open chalice or cauldron into which the mystical is poured for enlightenment. It is the receptive state of the Witch, and it is one in which the Witch comes to personal gnosis.

The voice of the wind is a teacher. We can and do learn from it, but it requires more than just this to educate the Witch. In Witchcraft balance is all-important and duality is part of the formula. We cannot know what it is we do not already know. Therefore, it is wise to use a variety of sources to hone one's Witchery. This includes traditional teachings, the time-proven and time-honored ways of those who came before us.

In the final analysis what lies in the heart and spirit of the Witch is of primary importance. You can learn a great deal, but it is who and what you are that determines the kind of Witch you are, and what you bring to the table. Therefore, developing your spirit as a Witch is key. There is an old saying in the Craft that we know our own. Be worthy of being known in your community and among your peers.

THE SHADOW'S EDGE

The concept of the shadow's edge is unrelated to the idea of shadow or shadow memory as the organic memory of the earth. Instead, the shadow's edge is a term for a particular in-between place related to light and blackness. In this case we are talking about a zone that is created by light falling upon a material object.

A shadow is literally, of course, an image of something blocking light. The shadow is formed by the light passing around the object, creating a solid black shape of the object. The shadow is what the light does not reveal about the whole nature of the object blocking it (no real details, just a suggestion of the form). In Witchcraft we view this as a metaphor for what is hidden and yet partially exposed. It is the edge between what can be known of the unknown.

In Old Witchery, this is tied to the concept of midnight being the witching hour. This also connects to midnight as the in-between place of magic in the night. We can imagine an edge of shadow and light on the meadow or forest floor. It is the threshold separating the exoteric from the esoteric. Here one must step across and enter the mysteries, for it is by choice and action that we may encounter the other side. Access to the shadow's edge is most effectively found at the crossroads, which is the ancient gathering place of Witches in the night.

On a magical level, what intrigues us is what lies behind the shadow. The light is what manifests the shadow, and for the Witch the night shadows fall under the reign of the moon. The moon itself seems to draw shadow across it as the phases come and go. In the Rooted Ways, Witches wear black robes (in part) to appear as shadows in the moonlit landscape. In this way they mystically connect with what generates their shadow, which is the power of the moon's light.

To illustrate the principle of the shadow's edge, consider the following. If I take a statue and use a candle to cast its shadow, the shadow is at first the projection of what I venerate through a representation.

The light that casts the shadow is the holder of, and is ultimately the source of, what is seen as shadow. Therefore, secondly, shadow is the edge between knowing what is hidden and greater and what is revealed to human understanding.

Following this, the statue is a means of being able to interface with the divine through a tool. Tools are important and empowering. They help us to literally wield a metaphor.

Some people feel that they reach a point in their magical career when they no longer need tools. This can be true, as I too have come to feel that I no longer need tools to work magic. By analogy, I don't need a fork and spoon to eat spaghetti. I could just push my face into the pasta and slurp it up. However, the use of tools (fork and spoon) makes the experience different and better. Yet, either method provides me with the nutrition I seek.

It is an interesting magical concept to think of a shadow as a manifestation of something as opposed to an image of what is blocking the light. In some ancient Egyptian writings, we learn that the soul (or some part if it) was carried in a person's shadow. It was therefore taboo to step on someone's shadow on the ground. Here we see a very ancient mystical connection to the shadow.

One old teaching from the '60s revealed the connection between the shadow's edge and the athame (or Witch's dagger). It was taught that, in essence, the athame is a "spirit blade" (as opposed to a physical blade), and as such it is never used to physically cut anything. Instead, the athame is primarily used to pierce the veil between the worlds and temporarily sever the bond that naturally seals it closed. The athame blade is double-sided, which represents the two realms: material and nonmaterial. The blade's edge is the shadow's edge, which in turn is the threshold between the worlds.

THE FAMILIAR SPIRIT

It is a very old idea that the Witch possesses a spirit ally known as a familiar. In the original concept the familiar is a spirit that can reside inside an animal such as a cat, mouse, frog, owl, or raven, or others. In modern Witchcraft many people regard a special pet as being their familiar. In most cases this is more of a "soul mate" idea than it is in keeping with the older model of a Witch's familiar spirit.

In the Rooted Ways a familiar is obtained by going to a crossroads on the night of a full moon. The Witch carries what is called an elf lamp or devil's torch. This is a black candle wrapped in a large mandrake leaf (page 89). The candle is placed in the center of the crossed roads and is lighted. A call is then given to summon a familiar spirit.

When we reincarnate in the material realm, we generate a resonance that is the soul vibration. There are things that are drawn to us as a result. One example is the power animal or spirit animal that can accompany us if we choose to work with it. Related to this idea is the familiar spirit except that it is drawn to a Witch. It is part of the spirit world of Old Witchery.

One of the purposes of the familiar spirit is to keep the Witch informed about matters concerning her or him. In some of the covens I practiced with, individuals would often be surprised that I knew various things about them without direct knowledge. This is because people would phone me and tell me various things. I always regarded this as the influence and inspiration of my familiar spirit. This was particularly true when the caller would voice that she or he probably shouldn't be telling me anything. People were compelled by the workings of my familiar. It is natural for the familiar spirit to automatically work on behalf of the needs of the Witch.

Another function of the familiar spirit is to protect the Witch from negative or adverse forces in both the material and nonmaterial realms. This acts much like an early warning system, alerting the

An elf lamp, made by wrapping a mandrake leap around a candle, can be used to summon a familiar spirit.

Witch to threats, danger, ill wishes, and magical spells cast upon him or her. The familiar can also guide the Witch into beneficial settings and to connections with others of like mind.

I personally find that the familiar spirit is effective to work with in the dream state. This allows for unencumbered interaction and interfacing. Placing the seal of "summoning the familiar" aids in this connection. The basic method involves putting the seal under one's pillow and speaking the invocation before going to sleep.

Placing the seal of "summoning the familiar" aids in this connection.

"I call upon the spirits Canas, Agar, Agla, and Rovon to open the dream gates, and to grant union therein with my familiar spirit."

CHAPTER FOUR

LINEAGE OR MAKING IT UP?

There are more things in heaven and earth, Horatio,
Than are dreamt of in your philosophy.

—WILLIAM SHAKESPEARE, *HAMLET*

In the 1960s and 1970s, there were people who claimed to be hereditary Witches from a long lineage. One famous Witch, Alex Sanders, claimed to have been initiated by his grandmother. He later went on to found what is now called the Alexandrian Tradition. Together with Gardnerian Witchcraft, the Alexandrian system was very influential in the establishment and growth of modern Wicca.

Individuals such as Gerald Gardner and Sybil Leek gave us the depiction of Witchcraft as a long-standing tradition, particularly in the New Forest area of England. It was a very popular idea in the 1960s and '70s that Witchcraft was a pre-Christian religion that survived into the Christian era. It was particularly popular among the hippie generation, as it suited their rebellion against established society. The idea of a counterculture that survived hidden over the centuries had great appeal. It was, at the core, a way of thumbing one's nose at mainstream society.

In contemporary Witchcraft there are those who argue that hereditary Witchcraft never existed prior to modern times. Others criticize or demean systems that continue to arise, negatively calling them "made up" traditions or systems. The truth is that any system or tradition was "invented" at some point in time. Personally, I prefer the term "assembled" over "invented," as I feel this is more accurate. What is most common is the assembling of older practices and beliefs into something modern in its application. This gives it the nature of something ever ancient and ever new.

There was a time when none of the traditions we know of today existed, including the very popular Alexandrian and Gardnerian systems. They had their origins, their assemblage, and their organized structure. This does not take away from their value and their usefulness for practitioners and followers.

As to how systems of traditions arise, I envision a time when early humans were taught by spirits or Otherworld intelligences of some form or another. There were those who, by some inner nature or predisposition, were acclimated and could *hear* spirit voices in some way. The tribe acknowledged them and accepted them, and these individuals were the prototype of the Witch, the shaman, and the mystic. More importantly, something from a nonmaterial reality also acknowledged these individuals, and communication began to flow back and forth. There is no true reason to believe that this process, this communication, no longer functions or is no longer used by contemporary Witches.

In this light we can say that so-called "made up" traditions/systems originate from the same sources and inspirations that our ancestors encountered in the past. In my book *Grimoire of the Thorn-Blooded Witch*, I pointed out that these transmissions are not an invention by an individual; they are a revealing to one from something outside. It comes through an alignment that establishes communication with beings dwelling in nonmaterial reality. I continue to recognize this tenet.

Another component to consider is the person who receives these transmissions. It is surely easier and more effective to transmit to an individual who is well seasoned in the Arts of Witchery. In this way the teachings make better sense, the receiver is well acclimated, and the understanding is in place from which to interpret things as intended. However, that being said, it has been my experience that spirits, entities, and the gods will use even flawed individuals as receivers of teachings. Judgment, it seems, is more a human thing than a divine one. By this statement I mean no offense to judgmental religions such as Christianity that teach adherence to a judging god who is to be feared.

In the 1960s, there was a story circulating about the Fool card of the Tarot. According to this story, the original Tarot deck had two almost identical cards—one at the beginning of the Major Arcana and the other at its end. The first Fool card showed the individual carrying a knapsack on a rod. The unlatched bag is completely flat, as it is empty. The other card depicts the same image of the Fool except that the knapsack is latched and full, as it now contains all the Major Arcana cards as personal experiences gained along the path. The teaching here is that the Fool and the Magician can appear to be the same on the surface by others. However, it is what the Magician carries within that distinguishes him or her from the Fool. In this same story we were told that the two jokers in a playing deck are witness to this old memory. This is not historical to my knowledge, but I simply pass on the tale.

The idea of what knowledge and experience are possessed by an elder is an interesting topic. It leads us to the concept of initiation. From a mystical perspective, initiation is a personally transforming ritual. It passes on to the initiate, by way of an energy transmission, the alignments that the initiator already possesses through her or his experiences and training. This bestows resonance upon the initiate, which opens her or him to specific beings that are drawn to its beacon. This increases and enhances the ability of the initiate to hear and be guided by the voice of the wind.

MYSTICAL INITIATION INTO WITCHCRAFT

Today, we have many different ideas about what initiation is and is not. In my own tradition of the Ash, Birch and Willow system, we use an older model than many modern systems. It is rooted in mystical concepts and occult principles of magic; but to where do these roots extend? Here we must ask how initiation first came about. In other words, who were the first initiators? What I can address here is what was passed on to me and what I continue to experience and see as true.

We know that in many early tribes or communities there were people who we now call shamans, witches, mystics, and so on. Perhaps it is fairer to call them the prototypes of these titled individuals. In any case, these were the people who spoke to invisible beings, who seemed to know things before they happened, who seemed to see things not of this world, and somehow communicated with all of this and with all of them.

The average person in the tribe or community was not like these individuals, and perhaps did not possess the mindset to be like these people. It seems natural that the "odd ones" in the community would tend to spend more time with each other than with other members of the tribe/community. This likely led to the formation of an inner society of like-minded individuals.

The origin story of initiation goes as follows. Certain humans caught the attention of spirits, and this is most likely because of something kindred; a resonance, if you will. This became a portal that allowed for communication. On the other side were voices willing to inform the seeker, and they whispered in the quiet times of receptivity. A connection strengthened humans, and spirits recognized that they both embraced the same things. A kindred connection formed through the love of the Greenwood realm, and when all sensed the moon's light as sacred, and when all understood nature as self-aware.

These were (and are) the stepping-stones that lead to the threshold of the Otherworld.

The seekers went on to intentionally cultivate a connection, to form intimate relationships with spirits of the land and the other side, and with spirits of moon and night. This resulted in profound influences and experiences. Such things were not inventions by individuals. Instead, this was a revealing to them from something outside themselves. It came through an alignment that established communication with beings dwelling in nonmaterial reality.

The many years it took to establish this connection, to sort it all out, to integrate it, became the condensed experience of the first seekers. They discovered the keys, the portals, and the connections to the Otherworld source. They explored them, charted them, and established a record of how this all came to be and how it works. These became, within the society, the inner secrets they shared with one another. To retain these connections on the material side of reality, they first used an object as the manifestation of the key to the portal (in other words, an interfacing tool). This was most often a cutting from a tree, which later became a staff, and later still became a wand. However, some used a stone, which later generated the idea of the Witch's ring, a ring with a stone setting.

Eventually, symbols were created to address and preserve the inner teachings. These were placed on the staff or wand to bind things together in a magical sense. The symbolism was only understood by those who knew the meaning, and what was behind the meaning. In time, people approached the fellowship and asked to be taught and to be trained. Through this the members of the inner society became the first initiators. These individuals had refined the processes that first led them to what they now connected with in the terms of the Otherworld. The way could be passed on to others now in a much shorter time than would be the case with seeking it on one's own. So they

In the caduceus, the initiator and the initiate are entwined around sacred knowledge.

trained individuals in the ways that they themselves had had passed to them; but more importantly, they passed to them the same energetic alignment that first attracted the spirit voices, the inner resonance.

In the oral tradition behind all of this is the teaching that initiation is a passing on (through sharing) of one's alignment to another person who is prepared to receive it. It is an intimate act, and it joins the initiator and initiate together energetically and etherically. There is always a flowing connection back and forth until it is intentionally severed. We can liken this to the image of the caduceus. In this light, the staff stands upright; it is the sacred record, the established way in. Entwined around it are two serpents, and here they represent the initiator and the initiate bound together. The wings above the serpents symbolize the alignment itself, the mystical power of initiation into the Inner Mysteries.

In the light of what has been presented in this chapter, initiation is a formal bestowing of a mystical force that is followed by specific teachings of the system that was the origin of that force. It is taught that the force is retained in the body of the initiator through being entwined in three body centers: the head, the heart, and the root. These correspond with the three meeting places of the entwined serpents in the caduceus.

This configuration is often called the Three Knots of Magic and they are activated through breath and touch techniques, and then the

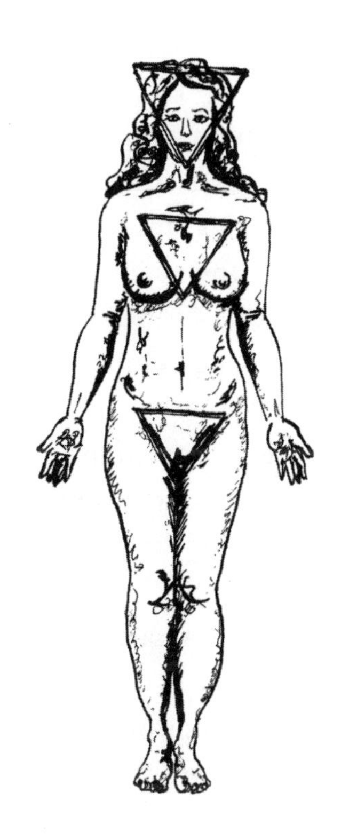

The three occult zones of the body, the head, the heart, and the root, can be activated through breath and touch techniques.

Oil of Initiation is charged by passing the breath three times directly into the oil. The initiate is then anointed with the oil, and in effect the power is passed to the initiate and a replica then resides in her or his body centers. This is not unlike the idea of DNA replicating and being passed on.

The presence of the Three Knots of Magic within the initiate maintains the resonance, and again this is the resonance that first attracted the spirits who taught individual humans. This presence reduces the need for sole reliance upon the initiator in the long run, for it becomes a beacon for Otherworld contact, and therefore a shifting to self-gnosis through spirit contact. Here the initiator becomes more of an experienced guide and mentor than anything else.

Initiations, in terms of the mystical or occult, are designed to cause a transformation. They are meant to induce a resonance that changes the relationship one has with what she or he previously held to be reality. Initiation opens the person to the enchanted worldview and its realization. A transformed initiate is recognized by Otherworld beings, which is one of the reasons why a new initiate is taken to each ritual quarter and presented in person by the initiator. It is, in essence, the initiator's statement that "I, who you already recognize and therefore accept, present this initiate, who is now the same lineage bearer." Think about the importance of that statement and relationship for a moment.

It happens from time to time that the relationship between an initiator and an initiate goes astray. Old legends are full of stories in which the apprentice betrays the teacher or the student assaults the master. When disharmony arises, it is healthiest for both parties that the bond of initiation be severed. Through the connective etheric cord, linked to the power centers in the body, the initiator sends the energetic *command* that unravels what is entwined. The cord between the initiator and the initiate is then magically severed. This breaks the lineage thread, and the force residing in the centers within the initiate begins to wither away. Once evaporated, all is as it was before the initiation took place in terms of the mystical connection/alignment. Lineage back to the origin is broken.

Some people will argue that initiation cannot be undone. Whether true or not, an initiator can certainly undo the alignments she or he formerly bestowed upon the initiator. If they can be passed on, then they can be removed. That being said, initiation is also something accepted by Otherworld beings associated with the system. The oaths sworn during initiation are accepted outside of the initiator's sphere of influence. In this light, breaking an oath is breaking a bond on all levels. Clearly this will result in consequences, and these may be permanent or at least long-lasting. This brings up the question, Does a deity, entity, or spirit care about giving one's word in an oath of initiation?

Unfortunately, initiates who are dismissed from the system into which they were initiated often refuse to accept personal responsibility for that action. Instead, they will blame their initiator and concoct stories that make themselves appear to be the hero in the tale (or they will play the undeserving victim role). This is a shame, because accepting personal responsibility is the one redeeming thing that can possibly resolve the true state of one's initiatory status as seen from "on high."

As to the idea of how a deity views an oath to it and to the tradition founded around it, the answer lies in the perceived need for the creation of an oath itself. In ancient times oaths were sworn to the goddess Hecate, and this traditionally took place at the crossroads. The person swearing an oath would kneel and place her or his hands on a hekataeon, which represented Hecate. To swear an oath to this goddess was considered to be unbreakable. A person may think the oath can be voided, but the goddess does not. This is why an oath means something and is not situational.

THE SOLITARY WITCH

Many people prefer to not be committed to a tradition, or to oaths of initiation, but instead to follow a self-guided path. Such a path is usually, but not always, an eclectic one. It is not uncommon for the solitary Witch to perform a dedication ritual, and in some cases, they may perform a self-initiation rite. However, from the perspective of the Rooted Ways, one cannot bestow initiation upon oneself. This is because we cannot give ourselves something that we do not already possess. Prior to initiation we do not hold the keys to initiation (as does our initiator). That being said, we can find our own way into initiatory understandings of the teachings and practices we seek and encounter. No secret is kept from one who truly endures, and no mystery is closed to an open mind.

Author Scott Cunningham (1956–1993) popularized the idea of self-styled approaches to practicing Witchcraft/Wicca as opposed to traditional methods. He wrote that the goddess and god would bestow initiation upon a seeker just for the asking. I cannot speak on behalf of deity, but I do have decades of experience with the theme of initiation. I believe there are generational differences as to the meaning of initiation. The old-school understanding is a personal commitment to a system or tradition. This is much like the idea of being fully committed to a monogamous relationship. The new-school view seems more about exploring one thing while waiting for the next. This raises the question as to why initiation is even viewed as worthy of attainment.

For some people initiation is a status they wish to possess, and to others it is a crossing over into a process of personal transformation. Many solitary Witches do not see any need for initiation, and they appear content to make their own way through the labyrinth. One of the blessings and challenges is that we have a choice. Without choice we are robots. It is important that our choices come from being informed.

Many people today think of a tradition as restrictive and confining. They feel it denies them their individuality and spontaneity. These people enjoy the freedom of drawing from different sources and using what best suits them at the time. But is a tradition actually restrictive and confining, or have we misunderstood its true value and mistaken it for something to avoid?

I like to use the following analogy. If I am a contractor and you want me to build you a house, I will do so using traditional methods of construction. In this way the foundation is strong, the walls bear weight properly, and the plumbing and electricity function as needed and expected. However, as a contractor, I do not tell you what colors to paint the interior rooms, how to decorate, what rooms to use for what, or how to live your life within the house. Instead, I simply provide you with a home and a place of sanctuary. It is there whenever you need to return to it or take advantage of it.

Over the past decades, I practiced several different systems and traditions. I also worked with eclectic materials. This provided me with the experience of both worlds as opposed to relying upon hearsay and assumption to form my views and opinions. This was important to me, and from this I drew an appreciation for the value of each approach and method of practice.

Today I teach and practice a tradition known as Ash, Birch and Willow. It is a noncultural system of Witchcraft that embraces the commonalities of European forms. I believe that when we strip away the cultural expressions and examine the core commonalities, we then come upon the oldest parts. These I call the roots or "rooted ideas" of Witchcraft. To distinguish them from purely modern ideas, I call the rooted ways Old World Witchcraft. Intentionally or not, there have always been the tenders of the Rooted Ways. From the rooted places spring forth the Inner Mystery Traditions that have stood the test of time.

Occultist William Gray once wrote something pertinent to what I want to convey in this chapter:

> *So what you are being given from the Inner Tradition is not the dead and mummified remains of previous superstitions, but a living, active, and authentic spiritual survival from our earliest existence on earth, which has been growing and changing through the centuries because it has been cared for and nourished by many generations of humans who realized the value of what they were entrusted with, and did their very best to ensure you receive it in a fit condition for furthering.*[1]

This ties into what is known in the Rooted Ways as the Well-Worn Path. Our ancestors cleared the way for us who follow in their footsteps. It then passes to us to clear the way further for those who walk the road we have extended behind us in our own time. The Well-Worn Path is the time-proven and time-honored methods of passing on the knowledge and wisdom of those who have done the needed work. To honor this, we must do more than cherry-pick from the teachings; we must study them in their cohesion and their collective body.

---

1 William G. Gray, *Western Inner Workings* (York Beach, ME: Red Wheel Weiser, 1983).

Being a solitary Witch allows the freedom to set one apart from community, system, or tradition if that is the desire. However, it does not negate the ties to Witchery that are inherent in accepting the Path. The timeless ways of Witchcraft do not give in to popular modern trends. Instead, they hold together that which can be drawn upon to support one's self-styled ways. The Old Ways tether the Witch to the soul of Witchcraft as opposed to allowing for the unrestrained freedom to become lost in the labyrinth of one's own making.

CHAPTER FIVE

THE OLD MAGIC

Hear now the words of the witches,
The secrets we hid in the night,
When dark was our destiny's pathway,
That now we bring forth into light.

Mysterious water and fire,
The earth and the wide-ranging air,
By hidden quintessence we know them,
And will and keep silent and dare.

—DOREEN VALIENTE, "THE WITCHES' CREED"

In chapter 1, we looked at the concept of the quintessence. The tools that enable the Witch to interface with the quintessence are the stepping-stones to reach Old Magic. Over time the tools of Witchcraft helped fine-tune the ways of practice. Along with this the settings in which to practice helped to attract, draw, and retain the energy of Old Magic in confined ways. These ways became a system, and some systems became a tradition of Witchcraft.

Among the many writings and Witch trial transcripts of Europe, we find a rich body of documents in Italy. In the seventeenth century Witch hunter Francesco Guazzo wrote in chapters twelve and eighteen of *Compendium Maleficarum* that Witches gather in circles drawn upon the ground with beech twigs, and work with spirits of earth, air, fire, and water (among others). Eighteenth-century Italian abbot Girolamo (Hieronymus) Tartarotti wrote in his work *Del congresso notturno delle lammie,* "The witches of our time are derived from, and are the offspring of, the ancient ones, who were followers of Diana, and Erodiade, and that their crime is witchcraft, just as it was in the past." He goes on to say, "The assembly of modern witches is nothing less than the ancient ones, and because of this succession they enjoy all the rights and privileges of their ancestors."

Writings such as these appear to address old and rooted themes in Witchcraft. It is the idea of something cohesive and coming from an earlier period. Lady Vere de Vere, in 1894, wrote an article in the June issue of *La Rivista of Rome,* stating that:

> *The witches in Italy form a class who are the repositories of all the folk-lore; but, what is not at all generally known, they also keep as strict secrets an immense number of legends of their own, which have nothing in common with the nursery or popular tales, such as are commonly collected and published. . . . The more occult and singular of their secrets are naturally not of a nature to be published . . .*[1]

Here we see the idea of Witches holding esoteric knowledge that is outside of the public arena. It suggests a measurable difference between contemporary knowledge and something from the past. There is, in this, something of the mystery of Old Magic itself.

When people speak of Old Magic, they refer to something mysterious and potent. The idea of something older than modern magic still clings within segments of contemporary Witchcraft. From this we can consider something as more "itself" than it is something we generate. It preexists us and it permeates the material world as well as the

---

1 Charles Godfrey Leland (as Hans Breitmann), *Legends of Florence Collected from the People* (London: David Nutt, 1895), xiii–xix.

nonmaterial realm. It is what first called the attention of our ancients as opposed to something they created on their own.

We can envision Old Magic as something drifting down from the moon and settling on the treetops where branches hold it in their embrace. We can liken it to the legendary mystical brew within the Witch's cauldron. It is timeless, sacred, and secret. Old Magic is not something we formulate in the common understanding of a magical operation. It *knows* what needs to be done in the evocation of its power. This is often why things manifest for us without having to do a conscious act of magic (providing we have established a direct connection with the Old Magic).

THE MEANING AND POWER OF THE PENTAGRAM

The five-pointed star within a circle is a very popular symbol associated with Witchcraft. It is commonly associated with protection but is also thought of as the symbol of the Witch. Wearing one can be a sign that the person is a Witch. However, there are older connections to the pentagram.

Within the occult societies of the nineteenth and early twentieth centuries, the five-pointed star symbolized the four elements of air, fire, water, and earth held in harmony with the fifth element of aether, or spirit. In this light the star represents the keys to creation within a magical system (and a spiritual system). In modern times many Witches have adopted the ritual and magical use of this star from such organizations as the Golden Dawn.

In chapter 3 we encountered the five-pointed star enclosed inside a circle as an old model. Here it represented the moon (and therefore the moon goddess) pregnant with the star-child. This mystical being is an integral part of the Old Craft.

When viewed through the tree branches, the stars can be thought of as "adorning" the branches. The branches, in turn, are antler-like in appearance. Here they become the crown of the Antlered God, who is intimately tied to Old Witchery. You will find more on this theme in chapter 8.

In chapter 1 we noted the moon tree in its trellis-like shape. The five-pointed star within the moon reflects the slats of the trellis, which symbolize the interconnectedness of all things.

The star-child weaves the seasons of the earth together, beginning with his birth on the winter solstice. In this regard, the year is the whole (represented by the circle). He (the star) traverses each month of the year within the circle (also known as the wheel). In doing so, he leaves the tracks of his footprints of his journey, which is the interlaced five-pointed star.

In this light, wearing a pentagram signifies that the Witch is in alignment and is synchronized with both the celestial and terrestrial tides. The five-pointed star symbolizes the flow and interaction of the elements that maintain the order of creation. These elements are available to the Witch, who can draw and direct them.

In the Ash, Birch and Willow tradition of Old Witchery, the star has additional symbolism attached to it. Here, the tips of the star represent thorns, which symbolize the efforts of the Witch to master the ways of Old Witchery. Witches in the Ash, Birch and Willow tradition are called Thorn-Blooded Witches because they have exchanged a blood oath covenant with the Spirit of the Land. The goal is to experience the thorns in pursuit of obtaining the rose (enlightenment).

Thorns are a natural protection, and the pentagram has a longstanding connection to protection. One old method of possessing protection is to create the Witch's ring, which was covered in chapter 1. The idea is set protective power into the ring, which can be raised and directed as needed. Afterward the energy is directed back into the ring.

THORN MAGIC

The use of thorns in Old Magic is an extremely old practice. In most cases they are used for protection, but they can also be used to cast a spell against an offender.

One practice was to place a bough over a doorway, threshold, or window. The belief was that spirits would not risk offending the spirit of the thorny branch. The thorns also presented the risk of an intrusive spirit being stuck with thorns. The primary thorns used in Witchcraft come from the blackthorn, hawthorn, and rose:

- Blackthorn thorns are small and relatively short. They are best used in pinning a binding, or in work with a poppet that is dominating or punitive in nature. This approach is sometimes needed to keep a foe from harming you or someone you love.

- Hawthorn thorns are long and very impressive. They are ideal for using with a poppet, as they can be inserted for healing magic or spell casting. Hawthorn is always used for gainful and positive works.

- Rose thorns are most commonly used for protection or for keeping something secret. In the Ash, Birch and Willow tradition, the thorns are mixed with herbs that are sprinkled around the edge of the ritual circle. This provides a barrier against anything of ill will entering the ritual setting.

In Old Witchery, before using a thorn, it is dipped into a fluid to align it with the nature of the work. For positive uses it can be dipped in honey. When dealing with an enemy or provoker, the thorn can be dipped in something sour or unpleasant. I like to use straight vinegar for this. If the work is for protection, then the thorn can be dipped in the juice of a hot pepper or in some hot spice soaked in hot water.

Once prepared, the thorn is verbally assigned an intention by the Witch. Then she or he may direct the thorns into a poppet (or in some other way connect the spell to a situation, place, and so on). The idea is to have the thorn be the implement that delivers the magical charge and its intention.

OFFERINGS

Placing offerings to one's deities is a timeless act of veneration. The classic offerings are grain (especially spelt grain), fruit, wine, and bread or cake. One classic offering to the gods and to faeries is equal parts of wine, milk, and honey.

When giving offerings to a deity, entity, or spirit, bear in mind the following. Whatever is put as an offering remains an offering until it is removed. Therefore, do not leave the offering to decay, gather mold, or become stale. If you do, then that is the current offering. This is something you will want to avoid because it can be regarded as offensive or sacrilege.

Once given and collected, the offering can be buried in the earth, consumed by fire, or dropped into running water. I recommend that you consider the environmental impact in your decision. We don't want to pollute anything with the offerings we need to dispose of from our acts of veneration.

There is an occult aspect to the giving of offerings after a ritual such as the Full Moon Rite. Traditionally wine is poured out (over the buried pentacle) to quench the thirst of the dead. Cakes are tossed up to the moon to connect it back to the Grain Mysteries. The round white cakes (or cookies) unite the moon and the grain, the goddess and the god.

PASSING VIRTUE INTO AN OBJECT

In chapter 1 we discovered the concept of the moon's virtue as an occult energy. We found that we can be imbued with this virtue and carry it within our mind, body, and soul. As Witches we are able to pass a portion of that virtue to an object or even to a person. This is useful for magically charging objects or doing blessings and healing work on other people.

This is easiest with the use of a virtue candle. The candle is white and the symbol of "descended virtue" is either painted on the length of the candle or etched into it with a needle or the tip of a blade.

To imbue the virtue candle with protective power, begin by lighting the candle. Look at the symbolism on the candle and reconnect with your feelings when you first drew virtue to you (as described in chapter 1). Make this as tangible as possible.

Next, kneel and say these words as you move the candle up from the bottom position of the triangles pictured in the illustration:

"I kneel to you,

I call to you,

I pledge to you."

A virtue candle, engraved with the "descended virtue" symbol, is useful for magically charging objects or doing blessings and healing work.

At this point the candle should be raised up over your head. Conclude by saying these words as you lower the candle back down to starting position:

"I reach you,

I embrace you,

I receive you."

Now, gaze into the candle flame for a few moments, and then touch your forehead and your heart area with the fingers of the left hand. You have now intentionally connected with the virtue within you.

You can pass virtue outward through breath or through physical touch (or both). This is performed by placing the fingertips of both hands upon your navel. Then slowly draw them up to your heart and bring them to rest on your lips.

Open your lips and draw in a deep breath. Move your fingers out a few inches away from your mouth and then exhale your breath onto them. Envision light pouring out and illuminating your hands. You are now ready to direct the energy of the virtue.

To use only breath, cup your hands as though you are holding water, and then blow your breath outward slowly across them. Direct this toward the target. You will do this three times, and before each breath you will say these words:

"May a portion of the virtue passed to me now pass to you."

At this phase you need to inform the energy as to its purpose. Think about your intention, and then add some words to convey it. For example, in a healing work you can say something to the effect of,

"May a portion of the virtue passed to me now pass to you. Receive and be healed of the malady with which you struggle."

When passing virtue to an object, you will customize the words to suit the intent. For example, if you want to bless a piece of jewelry, a crystal, or a tool, use the same method. However, this time you will inform the object as follows.

Hold the object in your left hand, say the following words, and then breathe upon the object:

"May a portion of the virtue passed to me now pass to you.
Receive my intention, [name it], and be filled with that power."

Conclude by squeezing the object with your left hand and declaring,

"So be it done."

If your work is performed through physical touch, the method of the breath and hands is the same one. The difference is that you will pass virtue through touch. This can be a massage or a laying on of hands. Use the same wordings as in the examples given in this section.

THE WITCHING CUP

The witching cup is a unique and important part of Old Witchery. It has several uses, including a magical alignment to the moon's celestial energy. Another use is to connect with other Witches in a ritual or magical work.

The witching cup is intimately connected to water, or more precisely to the moon's influence upon water. An ancient epithet for the moon goddess is "the dewy one" and this refers to the heavy dew the morning after the night of a full moon. However, we must also note the moon's effect upon ocean tides, and the moon's reflection on lakes and oceans. The witching cup symbolizes all these aspects.

The witching cup ties into the ancient teachings of the "mysterium lunae," which address the three phases of the moon: dying (waning), generating (waxing), and giving birth (full moon). These in turn touch upon the Three Great Mysteries: Where did we come from? Why are we here? And what happens after death?

To raise up the witching cup is to invoke the Mysteries. To drink from the witching cup is to satisfy one's thirst for a time from the well of the moon.

In the Rooted Ways it is said that into the cup is poured the mystery and hidden meaning of the starry night. Just as the moon receives, absorbs, and reflects light, so too does the Witch who partakes of the contents of the cup.

It is the sacredness of ritual and magical liquids and essences that empower the witching cup. There is an indwelling virtue within it, something transmitted by the divine feminine. It is here that we connect with the goddess of the moon.

The moon is sometimes called a giver of water through the auspices of the goddess. Dew is generated, which she directs to the earth, dripping from the moon, dripping from her. In occult terminology, the dew is "wet and warm" and mingles with the elements.

The goddess and her moon are "begetters of life" upon the earth. They bring the growth of plants and beasts and regulate the menstrual cycles of women, enabling them to become mothers. In this light, the goddess is the mistress over all waters/liquids and is the vital principle of all birth.

There is an old occult teaching of the Divine Source of Light from which all things were given birth. In this teaching the sun, moon, and stars reflect this light (each in its own way). Divine Spirit is the one light and is generated to the sun, which passes it to the moon. The moon passes it in turn to the raised witching cup. Here the Divine Spirit adds a virtue to the brew, and the soul (if it is spiritual) can take on the "glow" that is embedded in the liquid of the witching cup.

In the Rooted Ways the moon is the intermediary between the Divine Source and the shadowed earth. It works between the world of pure spirit of the fixed stars and the creative sensuality of the earthly elements that can distract us. The task of the moon goddess is to harmonize through the passing on of light.

In the Inner Mysteries, we find the teaching that the moon wanes in order for the goddess to replenish herself. This is a significant mystery in itself. That which gave virtue to all gave virtue to her. It empties her so that it can fill her once again. In this way it empties itself so that it can fill all things anew. The goddess then shows forth the light of the moon to share what is passed to her from the Divine Source. That light, as the full moon, is reflected upon the surface of the liquid within the witching cup. The goddess is mirrored in the cup, which is therefore rendered a sacramental vessel.

In the Rooted Ways the sphere of the moon is the gateway to the realm of the spirits to which the soul longs to return. The moon is suspended between the sub-lunar shadow and the changeless etheric light. Raising up the witching cup parts the shadow and invokes the light. It is then that the Witch receives the blessing of the goddess and is immersed into the light cycles of the moon. This, in turn, aligns the Witch with the cycle of birth, life, death, and renewal.

When moon and Witch unite, illusion and deception are dispersed. All things are then illuminated in the night. The witching cup is passed to all with these words:

"From the moon shines forth the glow

Of the night's celestial ray.

Her endless cycles show

To all their moonlit way."

For more details, see the section about the sacramental meal of the Witch's Sabbat.

THE WATCHERS

The concept of the Watchers in Witchcraft rituals has transformed over time. Today we see the influence of concepts associated with angels and apocryphal writings such as the Book of Enoch. This basic theme was popularized in Witchcraft books of the 1970s such as Paul Huson's *Mastering Witchcraft*.

In some magical systems, the Watchers are regarded as kings or lords of the four elemental realms. They have power over the quarter portals of a ritual or magical circle. Here we find Amaimon as the east Watcher, Gaap as the south Watcher, Corson as the west Watcher, and Ziminiar as the north Watcher.

The Watchers have a connection to the ancient stellar cults of what is now the Middle East. We saw them linked to certain stars, which in turn were connected to seasonal shifts on earth. However, there is another view, perhaps a more ancient one, about the Watchers.

Some of the tales circulating in the 1960s and 1970s depicted the Watchers as an elder race that existed before humankind. Their natural realm existed outside of material reality. They once had flesh bodies but lived well beyond the human life-span. At some point they entered the world of humankind and encountered primitive people. In this light, many myths and legends are based upon the presence of the Watchers.

Another popular tale is that the Watchers were a celestial race. Some stories called them the Lords of Karma. Their task was to observe and record the deeds of souls in mortal bodies. In this way each soul was traced from one lifetime to another, and through the efforts of the Watchers "cause and effect" were introduced into each incarnation from past lives.

Traces of this concept appear in old Witch lore, where we find the Watchers associated with cemeteries and the spirits of the dead that dwell there. In this context it is said that the Watchers help oversee the process of transition from life to death. On a deeper level they are also involved with the soul and reincarnation. In this light, they assist the soul in choosing a next lifetime as opposed to being subjected to it. In these roles the Watchers are known as the Gray Ones, the Hooded Ones, or sometimes the Shadow Company.

In the Rooted Ways, the Watchers observe the Witch in her or his rites and are present to witness initiation. This ties into the concept of being "properly prepared" to cross the threshold into initiation. To be acknowledged and accepted by the Watchers is to carry the auric imprint of an initiate. Other initiates can sense it and perceive that you are kindred.

In the teachings about the Watchers, we find that they guard the portals to and from the material world and the nonmaterial realm. Traditionally these are envisioned as marking the east, south, west, and north. However, they also guard the circle from above and below.

Nothing can approach the Witch's circle without notice being taken by the Watchers. In this same light, no noninitiate is granted access to the deeper inner realms without being recognized by the Watchers as a Witch. This is a safety issue and not a denial or some aspect of elitism.

The seal of the Watchers ...

THE SABBATIC MEAL

In the Rooted Ways the legendary Sabbat meal takes place during the full moon ritual. It has a religious connotation to it in terms of a devotional act associated with deity. However, its core meaning and symbolism are much older than modern ideas of religion and deity. We noted this in a previous chapter, which presented the concept of the fireflies and the Grain Mysteries.

In earlier chapters, we looked at ideas associated with the Sabbat meal. In this section, we will look at how the witching cup is configured in the ritual. It begins with the chalice and wine.

Ancient mystical legends reveal things such as a magical cauldron or a "holy grail" vessel in the form of a chalice. These symbolize what is worthy of obtainment. The stories also point to transformation through what is contained in these sacred vessels. The Divine Spirit is always central to the tales, and in them we find a goddess or a god associated with a vessel. Cerridwen with her cauldron and King Arthur's knights who quest for the Holy Grail are two examples.

In addition to the chalice, in the Sabbat meal we find the use of a platter. It holds the "cakes" that are part of the ritual. These items link us to the Grain Mysteries of birth, life, death, and renewal.

In essence, the grain cakes represent the slain Harvest Lord. They are his body as the seed bearer. Through his death the earth is reseeded for new growth.

The red wine represents the blood of the goddess, whether as menstrual or life's blood. The former is more often incorporated into waning moon rites, and the latter into waxing rites. However, the Sabbat meal is solely a Full Moon Rite in the Rooted Ways of Witchery.

In practice, the cakes are regarded as the substance and the wine is regarded as the essence. To consume them is to take their spiritual and magical virtues down into the cellular level of the body and upward into the soul consciousness. This combination creates an elevation of consciousness within the mind.

A specific method is used to activate the cakes and wine. Over each cake, using the Witch's blade, trace a crescent representing the harvest sickle. Next, trace an X over the cakes to symbolize the sacrificial death of the Harvest Lord. Point the tip of the blade at the cakes and say,

> *"By this sacred blade of the harvest, be these cakes the body of the Harvest Lord."*

Now the wine is activated. Pour the wine into the chalice. Position it so that the moon is reflected upon the surface of the wine. If this is not possible, use a lighted candle to represent the moon. Ideally, you will want to use the virtue candle.

Take a wand and trace a circle three times (clockwise) over the wine. Next, lower the tip of the wand into the wine, and say these words:

> *"By this sacred tool of the phallus of the life cycle, be this wine the blood and liquid essence of the goddess."*

To link all of this to the witching cup, drop a small piece of cake into the wine. Raise the cup upward and say these words:

> *"May the mystical light of the starry places descend into this cup, and through this may I come to realize that within me which is of the eternal gods."*

If you are working with others, then pass the cup around to each person. If you are alone, then simply drink from the cup alone. In either case, drink from the cup and envision the light filling your entire being.

THE WITCH'S BROOM

The broom is one of the simplest tools of Old Magic. In the Rooted Ways it is constructed of ash, birch, and willow. The handle is made of ash, which in old lore joins the Overworld to the Underworld (above to below). Ash grants mastery of the realms to the Witch.

The Witch's broom can aid with several tasks, including gathering a waft, cleansing a space, and swearing an oath.

The sweep of the broom is made from birch twigs. Birch has long been associated with spirits of the dead. With the birch sweep the Witch moves and directs these spirits. Here the Witch is the usher, not the master. However, the Witch can remove a haunting spirit even against its will through the power of birch.

The sweep is bound to the handle with willow strips. The willow tree is sacred to Hecate, and the symbolism of the willow strips on the broom is a covenant with the goddess. In this the Witch is bound by oath and heart to the goddess of Witchcraft. It is her power that enables the Witch to fly on the broom, which is a metaphor for traversing the magical Path.

GATHERING THE WAFT

One use of the broom is to gather the waft and direct it. To do this, you position the broom in a series of configurations. Begin by facing a cluster of trees at night so that you are looking west. Point the tip of the broom handle so that it points at the top of the trees. Then go through each of the following positions in order as follows:

1. Point the handle at the treetops, and then with the left hand, stroke the handle from sweep out to tip.

2. Place the tip down and pass your left palm upward across the birch sweep, from the willow strips and up.

The Witch's broom can aid with several tasks, including gathering a waft, cleansing a space, and swearing an oath.

3. Hold the handle with both hands joined together and bring them to touch your head and then your heart.
4. Present the broom outward and horizontal about waist high above the ground.
5. Point the tip of the handle down and bring it forcefully to rest on the earth.
6. Repeat the first two steps.

The movements of the broom are accompanied by a series of connective words, step by step. This is the chant:

"The limbs, the veins, the head and the heart,

the earth, the roots, the leaves and the bark."[2]

Here is how they are connected to the movements:

Point the handle at the treetops, and then with the left hand stroke the handle from the sweep out to the tip and say, "The limbs."

Place the tip down and pass your left palm upward across the birch sweep (from the willow strips and up) and say, "The veins."

Hold the handle with both hands joined together and bring them to touch your head and then your heart, and say, "The head and the heart."

Present the broom outward and horizontal (about waist high above the ground) and say, "The earth."

Point the tip of the handle down and bring it forcefully to rest on the earth, and say, "The roots."

Lift the broom up so that the sweep is in the top position, brush the sweep with your left hand, and say, "The leaves."

Conclude by pointing the tip of the handle at the treetops, and run your left hand along the handle and say, "And the bark."

The broom is now fully aligned and can be used to gather the waft. To do this, hold the sweep up toward the treetops. Move in a clockwise manner around in a circle and feel that the sweep is taking up some of the waft. Once gathered, you can walk around the edge of a ritual or magic circle and "shake off" the energy so that it falls into the perimeter of the circle. If you practice with a coven, you can pass the waft to each member individually. Have each person hold out his or her hand, left palm outward, as in an extended handshake. Walk

---

2 Song lyrics from "The Oak" on *The Quickening* by Spiral Dance, 2006.

around the circle and brush each person's palm with the birch sweep. This will pass a portion of the waft.

Cleansing a Space

Another use of the broom is to "thrash the air" prior to casting a circle when needing to cleanse a space. To do this, simply walk around the area and make sweeping/thrashing movements in the air with the birch sweep up above you. You can accompany this with words, if you desire:

"With the Witch's broom I thrash now the air

And disperse all ill-natured things residing there!

No evil spirit, phantom, or ill-wished bane

in the face of Witch wind can here remain!"

When done, place the broom over the door or in a corner with the bristles up for protection.

Swearing an Oath

Lastly, one important use of the broom involves swearing an oath. This ties into the ancient practice of swearing an oath to Hecate at the crossroads. A person would kneel and place one hand on the pole, a hekataeon. Next, she or he would speak an oath. This was usually performed during an initiation rite. However, it was also done in exchange for the granting of a specific favor.

In the Rooted Ways, the tip of the broom handle is pushed a few inches into the soil where the clay pentacle is buried (as instructed in chapter 1). The right hand is placed on the broom handle and the left hand on the heart. This is followed by speaking an oath. It concludes with pouring an offering on the soil over the buried pentacle.

WORKING WITH SPIRITS

In the timeless Arts of Witchcraft, the Witch works with a variety of spirits. Some of these are nature spirits, while others are elemental spirits (or spirits of the Otherworld). Once a person begins to work in earnest with Witchcraft, various spirits are attracted; they take note (as do the Watchers).

When working with spirits (or simply encountering them), it is wise to wear a pentagram. This can be in the form of a necklace, ring, or bracelet. As noted earlier, the pentagram holds a great deal of power and symbolism. It is no small matter to wear one.

In addition to the power of its symbol, the pentagram ties in a concept known as the "momentum of the past." This occult principle means that when something is done in the way it has always been done, century after century, it builds a momentum. Therefore, when something from the past is repeated in the present, it connects past and present together. From this the momentum of the past rises like a cresting wave and pours down into the act or gesture being performed in the present.

Therefore, the pentagram is far more than a symbol or statement. It is a living transmission of energy empowered by everyone who has ever used it throughout time. Spirits take notice of it and understand its power.

In Witchcraft, spirits are called or summoned in the night. The setting is typically a crossroads. There are two types of crossroads. In northern Europe, it takes the shape of an equilateral cross. In southern Europe, the crossroads is a Y shape. The triple goddess Hecate is strongly linked to the crossroads in Witchcraft.

While it is ideal to go to an actual crossroads at night, there is another way. You can use a cane or rod to etch one in the soil, or you can use a piece of chalk to draw one on a hard surface. Make the crossroads symbol at least three feet long.

In Old Witchery the goddess Hecate is addressed in order to inspire spirits to come to the aid of the Witch. Words such as the following can be spoken at the crossroads:

"Great goddess Hecate, you who control the gates between the spirit realm and the mortal world, I call to you.

"Hecate, you who aid the Witch's Craft, I call to you. Look with favor upon my enterprise, and open now the ways and grant passage between the worlds!"

The basic structure is to then etch a circle around the intersecting lines of the crossroads. Point your wand or athame at the direct center and then announce your purpose or intention in the summoning of spirits.

If you are working with specific spirits known by name, then summon them to appear. Give instructions to them as to what you desire to accomplish through their assistance. Once this is completed, remember to release them from the mortal world and call upon Hecate to usher them back. Conclude by asking Hecate to close the gates:

"Great goddess Hecate, I ask that you withdraw the summoned spirits back to their natural realm. Close now the gates between the worlds, and restore all as it was before."

THE LUNAR CHARGE AND THE ATHAME

The athame is a powerful tool and can be enhanced for spirit work by infusing lunar energy into it. This process begins three nights before the moon is full (the third night being the full moon).

Commence by digging a small hole in the earth as deep as your hand is long. Then take equal portions (about a handful) of the ground herbs vervain, moonflower, and jasmine. Add them to the soil from the hole you dug and mix this all together. Then replace the soil into the hole. Leave this until the night of the full moon.

On the night of the full moon, boil some water (about 8 ounces) to which you will add three pinches of salt. Then go out to the hole that you dug and slowly pour the boiled water out upon it. Next, mark out a triangle around the hole. Then place nine drops of liquid camphor directly upon the center of the hole. At this point, grasp the handle of the dagger in both hands, with the blade pointing down, and raise your arms up to the moon, saying:

"O' great goddess of the moon, bless me with power."

Then push the blade down into the soil (directly center in the hole) up to the handle base. Next, draw power down from the moon as follows:

Kneel before the moon, hands upon the thighs, and say:

"At will I call the streams to power,

from their fountains when sacred 'tis the hour;

seas swell and rest when clouds do I re-form.

With spells and charms, the serpents do I raise,

and from oak and boulder make known the ways.

Whole woodlands speak and lofty mountains wake,

portals open and spirits of the dead awake,

and thee, o' moon, I draw."

As you begin the last verse, raise your left hand and "cup" the moon in your palm. Then quickly close your hand in a grasping manner, seemingly closing the moon within your hand.

Do not look up at this point, but bring your closed hand down (as if drawing or pulling) and grasp the knife handle. Next, place your right hand firmly over your left and concentrate upon the knife, and imagine it glowing with power. After a few minutes remove the knife from the soil and clean it off with a white cloth.

The final process for charging the athame is to connect it with the earth and moon. Two days prior to the night of the full moon, bury the blade as prescribed. Take it by its handle in your left hand, and say these words:

"Seed to soil, death to birth, I join you now with the power of earth."

Then push the blade all the way down into the soil. The handle should be the only portion of the athame now above ground. Now it is time to leave the area undisturbed.

On the night of the full moon, you will return to the spot where you buried your athame and then perform the final step at midnight. Kneel in front of the athame and look up toward the full moon. Take hold of the athame handle with your right hand and hold your left hand up, palm facing toward the full moon. Next, close your right eye, look directly at the moon, and say these words:

"Beneath this light

that the ancients knew,

when time and season

and tide were true.

I call upon the ancient boon,

and with my hand

draw down the moon."

Then quickly close your hand as though you are grasping the moon. As your hand closes, look away so that you no longer see the moon in the sky. Bring your left hand down and cover your right hand with it, so that both hands now hold the handle of the athame.

Remove the blade from the earth, clean off the soil, and keep the athame wrapped in a dark cloth overnight. The athame is now ready to use for ritual or magical work.

THE WITCH'S DAGGER IN CIRCLE CASTING

In chapter 1 we encountered the athame as a tool associated with a star. The star connects the athame to the Watchers. In this light, the athame is used to activate each watchtower quarter around a circle. This is done by tracing a five-pointed star at each point, and then creating a five-pointed star on the floor of the circle. This establishes a pentagram image there, and the interlaced lines of the star connect to the perimeter of the circle. This pentagram protects the circle above and below, while the quarter stars guard the portals of the east, south, west, and north. The altar rests on the center of the star within the area shaped like a pentagon.

The use of the athame in activating the four quarters is as follows. Prepare a white candle; it will be used during the circle casting procedure. It will be carried around the circle, so be mindful of what size will work best for you (and secure it from dripping wax on the ground). When you are ready to cast your circle, place the candle on the altar and light it.

To begin, go to the east quarter. Hold the tip of the blade up to the night sky and point it toward the brightest star. Using your left eye, place the tip of the blade so that the star appears to sit on it. Look at this for a few moments and then slowly lower the blade while keeping your attention on it (avoid looking back up at the star). Envision that you are pulling the star to you from the night sky.

Carry the athame over to the altar and then, facing north, gently insert the tip of the blade into the candle flame. Envision that you are passing the star from your blade into the candle flame. At this point the candle flame is the light of the star.

The star flame candle is now used to evoke the Watchers at each quarter, beginning with the east and moving clockwise. To do this, simply trace a five-pointed star in the air as you focus on the candle flame. Start by holding the candle outward and up at head height. Move the candle down to your right hip, then up near your left shoulder and over to your right. Follow this by moving the candle to your left hip, and then back up above your head. Complete the pattern by lowering the candle and bowing your head in reverence. Repeat this at the south, west, and north quarters, and then

Using a virtue candle, create a pentagram to evoke the Watchers for help with your castings.

return to the east quarter. Here you will hold the candle up and give thanks to the Watchers for being in attendance.

THE WITCH'S RITUAL CIRCLE

In the Rooted Ways the circle is comprised of two sections: the inner and the outer. The inner circle is the boundary marker that designates the ritual area. Another circle surrounds the boundary, so that there are actually two concentric circles. The outer one creates a corridor between it and the inner circle. It is in this corridor that we are "between the worlds."

The edge of the outer circle is where the elemental gates stand, the portals that open to another realm. In some systems of Witchcraft these are called the watchtowers (of the Watchers). The gates make it possible for the energy raised in a circle to move out into the creative substance of the elemental realm. The elemental realm will, in turn, pass the energy on to the astral realm. This is where it will form an image so that it can later manifest in the material world.

All gestures, calls, and evocations are performed in the corridor and then ushered through the gates at the close of the ritual.

THE WITCH'S RING IN PROTECTION

Being a practicing Witch attracts attention on both the material and nonmaterial realms. This can be both beneficial and detrimental. It is important to know there are anti-forces that are opposed to the Witch just as there are allies who assist the Witch.

In chapter 1 the preparation and charging of the Witch's ring was given in detail. In this section we will add the "blue flame" protection to it. This is an enhancement, so be aware that the ring must be prepared before proceeding with the blue flame charge.

Begin by placing a large metal lid from a jar on your work area. Fill it half full with 180-proof grain alcohol or perfume or cologne. Slowly and carefully touch a lighted match to the surface of the liquid. A soft blue flame should dance across its surface. Attach the ring to a metal chain and suspend it over the flame. Gently swing the ring in a circle so that it passes in and out of the fire. While doing this, speak the words of enchantment three times:

"Fire, pass into this ring as a shield, flames of protection that do not yield."

Remove the ring from the fire, and then using your right index finger trace a five-pointed star over it. In your mind's eye, see this as a star of blue flame; sense it. Mentally pass the blue flaming star into the ring.

Next, hold the ring in the palm of your left hand. Take a lighted stick of incense in your right hand. Using the smoke trace a five-pointed star clockwise over the ring three times, each time saying,

"Strict charge and watch I give, that to the wearer of this ring, no evil thing approach or enter in."

This completes the magical charge. Whenever you feel threatened, hold the ring in front of you and say,

"Fire, rise from this ring as a shield, flames of protection that do not yield."

Mentally see it rise from the ring and sense its flaming presence in front of you. Place it between you and the menacing presence. Mentally enlarge the star as needed to match the situation, and then mentally move the star, pushing away whatever is in front of it. Remember to "reload" the ring with fire each full moon using the method of passing fire back into the ring.

THE CAULDRON

In Old Witchery, the cauldron is the vessel of magical energy. In the Rooted Ways the cauldron symbolizes several things. The raised handle is the Overworld (that which is above) and is what holds the celestial powers in place. The lid is the portal doorway that opens or closes the entryway between the worlds. The cauldron bowl is the inner world, the place of magic. The three legs on the bottom of the cauldron represent the goddess Hecate in her triformis or triple nature.

The Witch's cauldron symbolizes the Overworld, the inner world, and the portal between the two. It also represents Hecate in her triple nature.

To deepen the cauldron work, you can fill it with white flour, which brings the Grain Mystery element to one's magic and ritual. When the cauldron is filled with flour, you will note that by slowly sliding the lid across the mouth of the cauldron, the phase cycles of the moon appear in imagery. You will see a crescent followed by a growing "moon" until it is full in appearance. Moving the lid in one direction (right to left) will depict a waxing moon, while moving it in the opposite direction reveals a waning moon. In this way you can magically open a moon portal for ritual and magical use.

One example of using this method is to work for the gain or the release of something. Write down your intention on a piece of parchment paper. Read the words out loud and then set the legs of the cauldron on top of the paper. The symbolism here is that Hecate receives and holds the intention.

Light a stick of incense that is symbolic of your intention, and then use the smoke to trace a spiral around the cauldron. For works of manifesting something use a clockwise spiral, and for works to release (or dissolve) something use a counterclockwise motion. As you do this, recite these words:

> *"Goddess, who commands silence when secret mysteries are performed, I evoke you.*
>
> *Night, faithful keeper of my secrets, and stars who, together with the moon, take the night sky from daylight, I evoke you. Hecate of the three faces, who knows all my designs, and comes to help the incantations and the craft of Witches, I evoke you. Come, and look now with favor upon my undertaking.*

Pause for a moment and envision the desired outcome of your spell or work of magic. When you are ready, begin sliding the cauldron lid to represent the waxing or waning energy. As you do so, recite these words three times:

> *"The black, the night, the stars, and the moon,*
>
> *The earth, the seed, the light, and the womb."*

Next, pour some water over the flour in the center of the cauldron. This will make a dough-like clump. Reach in with your hands and compress the water and flour into a mass. Take it out and set it aside for a few minutes. Wash your hands and dry them.

The clump of flour and water can be used to convey the spell. You can place it on the property of the person in the spell casting, smear a thin line to seal an envelope, work it into the soil of your magical garden, or use it in any other way to make a physical connection. If that is not possible or desired, place the clump in a pan of water and boil it until all the water has evaporated. Do this on the waxing or waning moon, whichever is appropriate to the theme of your magical work. Bury any remaining residue.

One additional use of the cauldron is noteworthy. You can use the lid to heighten or subdue the buried Underworld pentacle used for libations. It is a simple method in which you place the lid over the area containing the buried pentacle. Turning the lid clockwise will increase the power of the pentacle, while turning the lid counterclockwise will lessen the activity in it. In most cases you will use the lid in conjunction with pouring libations. In this way you can formally summon and release the ancestors and the spirits of the dead.

WITCH'S HONEY

Witch's honey is one of the many things that has all but disappeared from the days of Old Witchery. Today it is most commonly used in love spells or spells to influence a person's mood. However, there are several older magical uses for honey.

The original concept is rooted in ancestral work. The teaching is that the ancestors exist in a group mind or "hive" mentality. This concept is symbolized by a beehive. This is where honey comes into the picture.

In Old Witchery, honey can be regarded as the "sweet essence" of ancestral lineage. We can extend this to a spiritual lineage as well. The fact that honey is sticky is a property that holds the generations together.

It is beneficial to make an ancestral honey jar. Simply select a glass jar (clear or amber) and fill it with honey. Insert a sprig of rosemary and one of cypress. Before putting on the lid, place both palms over the opening of the jar and say,

"From those before, the ways do pass,

the bonds between us will always last.

The one from many, our blood flows on,

Past and present join in the sweetest song."

Seal the jar and place it on your mantle or shrine shelf. Set a red candle next to it and light the candle when you wish to call upon your ancestors.

Outside of the ancestral connection, you can use honey for binding spells. This ensures that no harm is done. The spell uses honey to join lovers together, to stop misbehavior, and to attract your desires into manifestation. Methods include sticking photos of people together (face-to-face) with a smear of honey. You can also write your desire on paper and dab honey on the words to attract those ideas into your life. To stop ill behavior, draw jail bars on a piece of paper and then stick it on the photo of the offender with the bars facing him or her. You can also place this in your freezer to add an extra stopping power to the spell.

Anytime you perform a honey spell, say a few words over the honey to inform it of your intention. This can be done in a rhyming spell or simply freestyle wording.

In addition to these methods, a honey spell can be used to banish ill intentions, nightmares, psychic attack, and evil influences. To accomplish this, make a small jar of Witch's honey to set on your nightstand. Add acacia leaves to the honey and keep it open. Next, anoint a copper coin to set on each window ledge in your bedroom, and one on the threshold of the bedroom door. Finally, stick two copper coins together with a dab of honey and carry it in your pocket, your purse, or a pouch.

SKULL AND CROSSBONES

Among the most ancient tools of Witchcraft are the skull and crossbones. These are, of course, naturally associated with the spirits of the dead. In chapter 1 we looked at the use of the skull in communicating with the dead.

In Old Witchery the skull is a sacred cult object. Here it is known as the "skull of the first one" and is regarded as containing the remaining knowledge from the past. The reference to the "first one" relates to the idea of origin. It symbolizes the "first Witch" of ancient times, meaning the fount of our spiritual lineage (as opposed to the notion of a bloodline of descendants). One use of the skull in this way is to invoke the spirits of the dead into it as a means of bringing forth a recall from the past.

In the Rooted Ways the skull is prepared in a specific way. A gateway into the skull is opened by the four creative elements of air, earth, fire, and water. A red candlestick (representing the life of the blood) is set in front of the skull.

Holding the skull between both hands, an invocation is spoken:

"Breath of life the dead do yearn."

Exhale upon the skull.

"Body of flesh, the vessel of return."

Rap three times on the skull with the knuckles of the left hand.

"Fire of transformation, the bright, warm glow."

Light the red candle.

"The river of blood into the skull does now flow."

Hold both palms over the skull, then sit quietly and watch until the red wax begins to drip down the sides of the candle. This is regarded as the flow of Witch blood from the past into the present.

At this point the skull can be asked questions or called upon to give oracle messages. One simple method is the "yes or no" option. This requires two dried fava beans; one is marked with an X and the other with a circle. The beans are placed inside the skull, and it is then shaken until the beans fall out.

There will be four possible outcomes. Either the X or the circle will be faceup, or two blanks will show, or both symbols will display. If the X is faceup, it means no. If the circle is faceup, it means yes. Two blanks indicates that there is something being withheld in the matter, and it is wise to dig deeper. Both symbols showing means that the matter is not decided yet.

A more involved method of using the skull calls for someone to hold it while questions are asked. Typically, the skull will respond by feeling heavier for the response of no or lighter for the response of yes. If the holder of the skull possesses the ability of a spirit medium, then she or he can channel responses and speak with the oracle.

CHAPTER SIX

THE ART OF MAGIC

Magic has power to experience and fathom things which are inaccessible to human reason. For magic is a great secret wisdom, just as reason is a great public folly.

—Paracelsus

When most people think of Witchcraft, they think of magic. The idea of magic can be very alluring, and it often draws people to the practices of Witchery. There is a great deal more to Witchcraft than just magic, however, and it should be noted that a mystical force underlies all that is associated with the Path of the Witch. Magic is but one manifestation of this force.

A Witch is aware of an energy that can be used for works of magic. Magic is the use of this energy to manifest one's desire. This energy used by Witches can be thought of as the occult counterpart of atmosphere, as in the pervading tone or mood of a place or situation. It can be envisioned as an unseen mystical vapor that permeates all space, transmits transverse waves, and settles on all physical matter. It is the essence of what conveys magic.

In the Rooted Ways there are several terms used when referring to this magical energy. One example is to call it "the green mist." This term originates from the appearance of a green fog-like presence that is sometimes seen when a ritual or magical circle is cast on the ground in an outdoor setting. It gathers and slowly moves along the outer edge. This phenomenon gives us another name, "the verging."

There is an obvious connection here with the word *verges* as the indication of a border (and the word also applies to a hedge or the edges of a garden). Here we should acknowledge the related word *verdant,* as it means covered in green. The third connective reference word is the *waft,* and it is used in a less formal sense and has expanded meaning. This was covered in chapter 1, should you care to review.

The green mist is a mystical substance that is not sentient as we commonly understand the term. Assigning it a sentient nature would be to liken it to the ancient concept of *numen*, which is a belief that all things are self-aware. Instead, the green mist is a mystical substance that is receptive and pliable. The mind can impregnate it with a specific intent, shape it into a form such as a sphere, and then direct it toward the manifestation of one's desire or will. In this way the mist conveys the intention of a spell or other works of magic.

When we look at the green mist as "origin," it becomes clear that it is a preexisting source of power. We do not create it or summon it; it arises on its own. This is, perhaps, the thing that primarily distinguishes the magic of Witchcraft from that of sorcery and of ceremonial magic. In Witchcraft there is an organic component that blends with what the Witch invokes or evokes. In this the Witch is not controlling entities or forcing outcomes. Instead the Witch is participating in collaboration between the outer and inner forces that have influence in both the material and nonmaterial realms.

Witchcraft, as a system of magic and ritual, has its structures and methods. In my previous books I have written extensively on the components of magical formula. They are important to the working mechanism of magical Witchcraft. Therefore, I will include a version here for foundational purposes.

THE FIVE COMPONENTS OF MAGIC

There are essentially five components that comprise the art of creating successful and consistent works of magic:

1. Will
2. Timing
3. Imagery
4. Direction
5. Balance

WILL

It is the personal mental will of the Witch that drives the manifestation of any desired spell or work of magic. The will is, of course, the directed focus of the mind. The power of the will in any given work must be equal to motivation to accomplish your goal. The less intense the focus of the personal will, the less likely the manifestation is to appear. The stronger the need or desire, the more likely enough will power will be raised. This is one reason why magic should not always be the first remedy to a need or situation. Magic should be a resource in times of need as opposed to a commonplace practice. This keeps it sacred and powerful.

When applying the will, it is important to not let your thoughts stray. If they do, you can unintentionally morph the effect you desire to manifest. This is one reason why written evocations or invocations are useful to keep things focused on the intent. Rhyming words in one's spell is effective in keeping the train of thought fixed in place.

TIMING

In the performance of magic, timing can mean success or failure. Witchcraft is rooted in the ways and cycles of nature. The night is the preferred time for the Witch's magic because calmness has settled over the hectic energy of daily life.

The best time to cast a spell or direct a work of magic is when the target is most receptive. Receptivity is usually assured when the target is passive. Therefore, an effective time to cast a spell is when people are asleep; corporations are closed overnight and on holidays, and so on. In this way there is no counter flow of energy there to buffer the spell. Another important factor is to take into account the phase of the moon. Always work with nature and not against it. Generally speaking, 4 a.m. in the target zone area is the most effective time to cast a spell of influence over a person or a situation.

IMAGERY

The success of any magical work also depends upon images that connect the Witch to the desired manifestation. This is where one's imagination enters into the formula. The image you use should heighten your emotions and draw you deeply into the work at hand.

Anything that serves to intensify the emotions will contribute to success. Therefore, things such as a drawing, a statue, a photo, or a symbol are very useful. For increased energy you can accompany it with a scent, article of clothing, sound, or setting that adds to your connection. The merging of these components will greatly add to your successful outcome.

Imagery is a constant reminder during the spell casting of what you wish to attract or accomplish. It acts as a homing device in its role as a representation of the object, person, or situation for which the spell is intended. Imagery joins with the personal will to shape and direct everything in accord with the will of the Witch. This becomes the pattern or formula that leads to the realization of desire. Surround yourself with images of your desire and a resonance will arise, forming a directed vibration that will attract to you the thing you desire.

Direction

In order to have any outside effect, magic must be directed in accord with time and space. Time, space, and energy are the three points of manifestation. This principle is called the triangle of manifestation. It is active now in your hands because you taking the time to read this book, you are in a space/location, and you are putting forth the effort to read these words.

Releasing magic is necessary for it to have an effect on anything outside of oneself. Once energy is raised, you must direct it toward a space/location. This connects you and the target by a cord or bridge of magical energy. It is through this connection that the desired results of your spell will return to you.

Once you release the magic of the spell, do not be anxious concerning the results. Anxiety will act to draw the energy back to you before it can take effect. Reflecting upon the spell tends to ground the energy because it draws the images and concepts back to you. Once you cast a spell, it is best to not give the matter further thought so as not to drain off its effectiveness. Mark a seven-day period on your calendar and evaluate the situation seven days later. It usually takes this amount of time (one lunar quarter) for magic to manifest.

Balance

As with all things in Witchcraft, balance is essential in a spell or other work of magic. Balance is about knowing the outcome in accord with what is realistic. Therefore, you need to look at what you are trying to make happen and the reality that surrounds it. As a mundane example, you can't make roses grow outside in the snow. When casting a spell, know the greater forces already at play and then design your magic to match and work within that reality. Balance is joining in with the tide and the flow.

Another element related to personal balance is to consider the need for the work of magic as well as the likely consequences on both the spell caster and the target. If anger motivates your magical work, then wait a few hours or sleep on it overnight. While anger can be a useful propellant for a spell, it can also cloud the thinking. Again, it is a question of balance. In my personal practice of martial arts I learned not to let anger or fear of pain into the situation of any encounter. Purity of focus and energy is vital to the desired outcome; everything else is counterproductive to success.

Balance also calls for you to make sure you have exhausted the normal means of dealing with something before you move to a magical solution. Make sure you are feeling well enough to work magic, and plan to rest afterward. Magic requires a portion of your vital life-force essence. Replenish this with rest even if you do not feel tired.

THE FOUR ELEMENTS IN MAGIC

In the realm of magic and ritual we find teachings regarding four mystical creative elements. These are called earth, air, fire, and water. They are used for various purposes in the art of ritual and magic. The most common usage in modern Witchcraft is the creation of a ritual or magical space. This is known as the circle of the arts (in which practitioners gather to perform magic or ritual). Additionally, the four elements are used to empower spell casting and other works of magic.

The idea of the four elements of creation is rooted in the concept that everything on the physical plane has a nonmaterial counterpart. This concept belongs to the field of metaphysics, which is a philosophy concerned with the fundamental inner nature of reality and being. According to the teachings, the four "building blocks" for creation existed before anything did of a material nature. The oldest writings on this subject happen to come to us from ancient Greece in the form of a myth. The ancient Greek known as Empedocles is credited with revealing a cohesive understanding of the four elements through formal teachings, such as his Tetrasomia, or Doctrine of the Four Elements.

The early myth of creation depicts the universe in chaos. Only the elemental forces of earth, air, fire, and water occupied the great void. Each of the elements was separate and independent. They did not work together, and there was no purpose and no direction. All was in disorder. Because of this condition creation was not possible. This setting was called chaos.

The myth goes on to tell us that in the midst of chaos, the fifth element of spirit appeared. Ancient text refers to it as aether, and this is often thought of as the Divine Mind. The fifth element drew the forces of earth, air, fire, and water together into harmony. Each became an integral tool for creation, and once the elements were unified the worlds were created through divine direction.

In elemental magic, the four elements are called upon to create a mini-universe, which emerges from the process of casting a circle for ritual or magical purposes. As the Witch casting a circle, in effect you become the fifth element and bring the elemental forces together in unison. These forces give form and vitality to the created space. They also energetically mark out the boundaries of the circle, which serves as a place set apart from the everyday world, among other functions.

Now that we have looked at the elemental forces, let us examine each of the separate elements.

EARTH

In magical terms, elemental earth is the cohesive and condensing force. It is the anchor of manifestation. The element of earth provides and maintains the stability that is required for things to take form and to manifest in the material plane. In the art of magic, the elemental earth force is associated with the tool known as the pentacle.

In modern times some systems assign the color green to the earth as a correspondence for ritual and magic. This is likely due to wanting to assign the color of earth's vegetation to the earth itself, whose soil color is brown in most cases. An older assignment comes from viewing the sun's light and warmth as the agent that awakens and sustains the vitality of the earth. In this light the color yellow symbolizes the earth, a reflection of the vital essence that awakens fertility in the earth. Most systems assign the element of earth to the north quarterly direction in a ritual or magical circle.

Traditionally, each element has a tonal assigned to it that aids in its activation. The tonal for earth is the letter *A*, and when spoken it is stretched out and carried upon the utterance: *a-a-a-a-a*.

AIR

In magical terms air is the transmitting elemental force. It carries or conveys one thing or another. This connects elemental air with communication. In magic, air is often used to "inform" something by passing into it a magical intention. This is a form of "charging" an object through magic.

In the Art of Magic, the elemental air force is associated with the tool known as the wand (some systems assign air to the athame). In the case of the athame, one association is that the blade cuts through the air. In the case of the wand, the association is that the wand was once a branch moved by the wind. I was taught that a tool should not be able to be destroyed by the element it represents, which is why I use the assignment of air to the wooden wand, as opposed to fire.

In modern times, most systems assign the color yellow to air as a correspondence for ritual and magic. This seems to arise from the association with the idea of the sun in the sky. The older tradition assigns blue to the sky (because the sky looks blue in daylight). Most systems assign the element of air to the east quarter in a ritual or magical circle.

The tonal for air is the letter *E,* and when spoken it is stretched out and carried upon the utterance: *e-e-e-e-e.*

Fire

Fire is the element of transformation. Whatever fires touches it changes. Set fire to paper and the result is ash. In this regard, fire can create and it can destroy. Fire allows for metal to be forged into a tool, and it can likewise melt one into liquid (without destroying the substance itself).

In modern times, most systems assign the color red to fire as a correspondence for ritual and magic. This is because fire makes things red-hot. Most systems assign the element of fire to the south quarter in a ritual or magical circle.

The tonal for fire is the letter *I,* and when spoken it is stretched out and carried upon the utterance: *i-i-i-i-i-i.*

Water

Water is the element of motion or movement. It is also a purifying and dissolving element. In this sense it removes the previous state of being. Water can be seen as that which is changeable, as opposed to earth, which is the enduring and stabilizing force.

In modern times, most systems assign the color blue to water as a correspondence for ritual and magic. This seems associated with the color of the sky reflected on the surface of the water, which makes the water look blue. The older assignment is green, which is how stormy water appears. This represents its power as an active force.

Most systems assign the element of water to the west quarter in a ritual or magical circle.

The tonal for water is the letter O, and when spoken it is stretched out and carried upon the utterance: *o-o-o-o-o*.

THE ELEMENTAL TOOLS

In modern Witchcraft we find the four tools of Western occultism, which are the pentacle, the wand, the athame, and the chalice. As previously noted, they symbolize the four creative elements of earth (pentacle), air (wand), fire (athame), and water (chalice). Let's begin with the earth tool, the pentacle.

THE PENTACLE

In the magical arts we find the altar tool known as the pentacle. It represents the material realm as well as the element of earth, or more precisely the elemental force of earth. Traditionally, the pentacle is made of clay, stone, or metal. These materials come directly from the earth, which thereby links the tool with the elemental nature.

The origins of the pentacle may lie in primitive use of gourds, which in turn were displaced by wooden platters or flat rocks. We know, for example, in the ancient cult of Mithras that a platter was used as one of four ritual tools. The others were a cup, a wand, and a metal blade. A scourge and "sun whip" were also used in the cult, and collectively these tools resemble those appearing centuries later in Gardnerian Witchcraft.

The pentacle, in its connection to the element of earth, is a tool primarily used for the purpose of manifestation. In connection to this theme the tool is also used to make a declaration in terms of the magic or ritual work at hand. For example, once a ritual circle has been cast, the pentacle can be carried around its perimeter while declaring the circle to be set as a barrier, container, and protection.

The pentacle can also serve to open and close gateways or portals at the four directional quarters of the circle: north, east, south, and west. In this usage the pentacle is held in the hands and pivoted like a door. Moving or swinging the pentacle away from you is an opening gesture, while moving it toward you is the gesture of closing. Focus on the sensation of a physical door opening or closing.

As an altar tool, the pentacle is often marked with the magical and sacred symbols of the group (or solitary practitioner). This serves to connect the material with the nonmaterial realms (the physical and the metaphysical). This embraces the concept of "as above, so below" in that the symbols unite what they represent in terms of earthly adherence. In other words, the symbols represent the spiritual markers of the group or individual, and reflect them into the ritual setting, and the mindset of the practitioners. One example is the pentacle that is often ascribed to Gardnerian Witchcraft.

In Gardnerian Witchcraft, a center star in the pentacle represents the four elements under the influence of the fifth element known as aether (spirit). This speaks to the power of manifestation in accord with personal will or desire. It signifies the pentacle as a tool whereby form is given and maintained. Above the star, from left to right, are the symbols of the degrees of initiation. These are the levels of attainment in understanding the ritual and magical arts. Near the lower tips of the star appear the symbol of the divine masculine (left) and the divine feminine (right). These unite the symbolism of the pentacle with the concept of fertility, which in turn allows for manifestation. Beneath the star appears the symbol of the kiss and the scourge, which denote passion and endurance. These are signs of devotion and dedication as well as catalysts to altered states of consciousness.

From a spiritual perspective, the pentacle is symbolic of the shield carried by the spiritual warrior. In this context it is sometimes called the shield of valor. The idea here is that personal ethics and knowing who you are provide the strength of character necessary to persevere on one's path. Nothing can undo or take away a steadfast position that is built upon a strong and true foundation. In this sense the pentacle is an outward sign of the practitioner as an unconquerable guardian against all that is unbalanced, untruthful, and deconstructive.

Charging the Pentacle

In chapter 1 we encountered a pentacle that was buried in the ground. In this section we will look at the classic pentacle used largely on the altar. There are several ways to use the pentacle in magic and ritual. Naturally, you will need to obtain or make one for yourself. It is most effective to use one made from clay or metal. However, a wooden pentacle can also be effective with the right alignment to its earth connection, which is tied to the Greenwood realm of nature. Avoid synthetic materials.

Ideally, your pentacle should be no larger than a standard dinner plate and no smaller than a saucer. The pentacle needs to have a pentagram marked upon it. As previously mentioned, this connects it to the four elements, and as an elemental tool the pentacle commands from the material plane. In other words, it serves you in the manifestation of your intentions.

Once you have your physical pentacle, take it outdoors at noon. Cover it with a thin layer of soil (potting soil is fine). Around the pentacle, mark a triangle using either pebbles or lines of soil, enclosing it in the center of the triangle. Next, place the palms of both hands over the pentacle and say these words:

"I declare this pentacle to be a tool through which the forces of elemental earth can be attracted, drawn, focused, and wielded."

Next, trace a triangle on the ground with your left index finger. Then focus your attention on the element of earth. Sense your body becoming solid and firm like a boulder.

Breathe in deeply three times, and sense this feeling become stronger each time. Now it is time to pass this vibration into the pentacle beneath the soil. To do this you will give a tonal, the sound of the letter *A*. Direct the sound of your voice through the triangle and into the pentacle. Begin by saying the following words:

"By the tonal of earth, I pass into this pentacle the quality of earth, and I establish the principle of like attracts like. Thereby I create this elemental pentacle of earth."

Now sound the letter *A*, stretching it out in your exhaled breath in this manner: *Aaaaaaaa*.

Lastly, trace the entire star on the pentacle clockwise from its upper tip and back again, saying these words of empowerment:

"Strict charge and watch I give, that in the presence of this pentacle, nothing evil, negative, or imbalanced may approach or enter in."

Remove the soil from the pentacle and wipe clean. It is now ready for the altar. Recharge the pentacle on the full moon to keep it vital.

Using the Pentacle

In this section we will look at several ways to use the pentacle in ritual and magic. To begin, let us consider its use in casting a circle. Prior to setting your circle, carry the pentacle around the perimeter, beginning at the north. As you move around the circle clockwise, hold the pentacle out in front of you with both hands. Face the star symbol away from you and toward the outside of the circle area. Say these words as you pass around inside the circle area (one full and complete round):

"Behold the pentacle, wielder of elemental earth. What is cast this day is bound this day, as above so below."

This announces that the circle is to be set in accord with the force of earth and will hold the properties of protection and containment.

Once completed, set the pentacle on the altar. After you have finished casting your circle per your method, you can use the pentacle to open (and later close) portals to the four directions. This is accomplished by going to each quarter, beginning with the east, and holding the pentacle outward to the rim of the circle. Think of this posture as though you are holding the hatch to a round window on a ship. The hatch swings out to open the view and inward to close it. Use the pentacle in that manner. Be sure to always close any and all portals that you open.

When using the pentacle as a hatchway, you can say words to this effect:

"By the power of the pentacle, I open this portal between the worlds, and connect the world of mortal kind with that of the Otherworld."

To close the portal, say:

"By the power of the pentacle, I close this portal between the worlds, and disconnect the world of mortal kind from that of the Otherworld."

The pentacle can be used as a focal point that serves to bring about manifestation on the physical plane, like a magical platter. To use it in this way, place an object that you wish to empower or enchant.

The pentacle represents manifestation and is like a homing device for elemental earth. One example is the charging of a ring for some magical purpose, such as protection.

Place the ring on the center of the pentacle. Speak these words of enchantment as you trace the entire five-pointed star on the pentacle from the upper tip downward to the right and follow the lines back again to the upper tip of the star:

"I evoke the essence of Divine Spirit and invoke its protective nature into this ring."

Then trace the entire star from its earth position up to the tip and around the entire pentagram back to the earth position, saying:

"I evoke the essence of earth, and I invoke its fortifying nature into this ring."

The pentacle can also be used to bind something from action. For example, one might want to stop a person from harming another (either through mean-spiritedness or physical abuse). To do this, take something that links to the person, such as a photo, clip of hair, item of clothing, jewelry, etc. This will be placed beneath the pentacle for one full cycle of the moon, beginning as the moon wanes.

Begin by placing the pentacle on the left side of your altar, and the object to the right. Trace the star from the earth position and back again, saying,

"I evoke the power of earth to bind, to enclose, to cease activity."

Next, pick up the pentacle and hold it over the personal item and say,

"I direct the power of earth to bind you, enclose you away from [name the person or situation], and stop your actions."

Then slowly lower the pentacle down onto the item. Do this with focused intent and deliberate intention. Use words to this effect:

> *"The weight of earth overpowers you, holds you still, ceases your ill intentions, and stops your harmful actions. You are held bound from harming others. Be still, be silent."*

Leave the pentacle in place until the moon is full, and then remove the object beneath it. You may need to repeat this if problems persist.

The Wand

The wand is among the most ancient tools used by ritualists and magicians of the past. It has a rich history that will be explored in this section. Ancient classical writings depict Witches such as Medea using a wand for magical purposes. Over the centuries the wand is depicted in relationship to the wizard and sorceress as well. Among the earliest mentions of wands we find that the wood used for them comes from the beech tree.

There is an archaic spiritual tradition associated with trees (and by extension with wands). It is connected to the sacred groves venerated by our ancestors. Tree worship was widespread among ancient people. Each grove contained a sacred tree that was the center of the cult. Its branches held special meaning, as is evidenced by ancient tales of the sacred bough. One example is the silver bough of northern European lore, which is connected to the faery realm. Another example is the golden bough of southern European lore, which is associated with the Underworld. In this lore the "needed thing" in order to successfully complete a quest is provided through magical means associated with a tree.

To carry a sacred bough was to wield the power of the force, entity, or deity within it. Therefore, it was considered essential to establish a personal rapport. In associated lore the priestess or priest trained in service to the inhabitant of the sacred tree. The years spent in this way came to represent the measurement of her or his devotion, service, alignment, and rapport. Once a period of time was served, the priestess/priest was allowed to take a branch from the tree. This branch became the staff, a sign of mastery and devotion.

The branch reflected the skill of the priestess/priest. It was cut to match the height of the individual plus the length from the inside of the elbow to the end of the tip of the middle finger. The former symbolized the experience of the priestess/priest, while the latter represented the service of the priestess/priest extended to others in the community. To extend, the arm moves forward from the elbow, stretching the hand outward. This is the inner symbolism and indicates one who is of the priestess or priest Craft. In this way the wand is the bridge to and from the Divine Spirit through the conduit of those in service.

According to old lore, when the one god came to displace the many, the Old Ways went into hiding. Over time the staff diminished into the wand, still retaining its symbolic connection to the sacred grove and to its divine nature. This is one of the reasons why the wand is traditionally made of wood, for this is the rootedness of its lineage. In contemporary wands, some practitioners choose to use wands made of metal, stone, or other substances.

The Elemental Nature

In some systems, the wand is assigned to the element of fire and in others it is associated with air. The assignment of fire may be rooted in the ancestral knowledge of using friction on wood to ignite a fire. The old lore held that fire was inside wood and could be evoked from it. Later in time a glass lens was used to coax out the fire. This was one method of passing the divine flame of a grove from one site to another. To accomplish this, bundles of branches were carried off to another area, and these served to pass on the original sacred fire from the sacred tree, as well as supply torches for the new grove.

Now let us look at the alternative elemental alignment. The assignment of air with the wand is rooted in the nature of the branch, which swayed in the breeze. The branch was also the resting place of birds (creatures of the air) and a site for their nests. In the mystical sense, the wand is coaxed to "remember" its movement in the wind and thus become animated by air.

In some systems the wand is connected to the mental will of an individual; in others, it is the intuition. The wand is directional in its concept and is connected with elemental forces that evoke and invoke. This theme ties in with the principle of the mind's ability to visualize thoughts that can become forms. This is reflected in the imagery of the Magician card in the Tarot.

The Magician, in Tarot symbolism, is connected to Mercury, the planet and the god (aka Hermes). The wand of Hermes is the caduceus, the rod with two entwined serpents. Hermes was, among other things, the messenger of the gods bearing his "wand of miracles." As such he was the transmitter and channel, which is still reflected in the essential elemental nature of the wand.

In ritual, an altar is the focal point of the circle, which is in and of itself the microcosm of the universe, the Magician's world within the greater world. Here the Magician calls up the four elements and creates a sphere that contains the forces drawn to it or raised within it. It is part elemental force and part material resonance. It is literally between the worlds.

In the Tarot imagery, the Magician raises his wand upward to the heights with one hand and directs his intention downward to the depths with the other. Upon the altar is the staff (along with other tools of the Art). Here the Magician stands as the sacred tree bearing the branch that is his measure.

Ritual and Magical Uses of the Wand

The wand has a variety of uses in ritual and magic. It can be used to cast a circle with, control open portal activity, direct energy that is drawn or raised, and pass blessings to a setting, person, or group of individuals. In this light it is also used to bless ritual cakes and wine on the altar. All of this is connected to the link between the divine and the wand, and its nature to be a bridge or conduit.

In a ritual circle the wand can be used to announce the beginning or end of a rite. This is done by simply knocking on the surface of the altar with the end of the wand. Traditionally, three such knocks are sounded. The same technique can be used to declare that a ritual or magical circle has been properly cast. In essence, the wand represents the authority of the Divine Spirit.

As a tool of authority, the wand can be raised upward or outward to command. It can also be carried around a ritual or magical circle that has been cast to enforce the nature of the circle as a protective barrier. In its magical aspect, a wand held horizontally blocks or signals a stop, while one held upright allows entry or passage. This makes the wand effective in front of open portals or gateways left temporarily open into the ritual circle.

Another aspect of the wand is its connection with the theme of fertility. If we picture a mortar and pestle set, we can liken it to a wand and chalice. In a ritual and magical sense, the wand is a phallus and the chalice is a womb. Inserting the wand into the chalice is an act of procreation, a ritual or magical act designed to impregnate and bring forth offspring. The offspring, in this case, is the end result of a spell or the manifested intention of a ritual.

For the blessing of ritual cakes and wine, the wand is used to trace a symbol over the sacred meal. This symbol can be unique to the practitioner (with symbolic significance) or can be something general like a crescent for lunar blessings and a circle for solar. The presence and manipulation of the wand awaken the spiritual essence of the wine as the blood of the divine feminine, and the cake as the flesh of the divine masculine. In some systems this is reversed.

Symbolism and the Wand

Various symbols can be placed along the sides of the wand. Ideally, these should include symbols of deities and spirits that the practitioner works with in ritual and magic. Other symbols can include elemental connections.

With the wand held in hand, the symbols become affirmations and alignments flowing through the consciousness of the wielder. Symbols are a type of "sign language" for entities on the other side. They not only convey intention and the source of power connection, they also become energetic thought-forms. In other words, they have effect through the power they represent, and thereby a reaction to them is made manifest.

The symbols for the wand can be painted, carved, drawn, or even burned on with a wood-burning tool. While placing each symbol on the wand, focus your mind on its meaning. Once in place, trace your finger over the symbol and verbally declare what it represents.

Charging the Wand

In this section you will find two methods of charging the wand. One method is for aligning the tool to the element of air, and the other to the element of fire. Simply choose which element you feel the most connected to in terms of the wand, and then use the corresponding elemental charge.

To Charge by Air

To charge by air, light a blue candle and some incense with a flowery scent. Pass the wand through the flame three times, each time saying these words:

"Through the transformational force of fire, I change this tool from a mere physical item into a magical implement."

Now, stand with your wand in your left hand and your feet together and arms extended, so that your body forms a Y. Imagine you are a tree, and then gently move your arms like branches swaying in the wind. Try to connect with this feeling of moving air that is causing you motion. This will establish a connection between you, the wand, and the element of air.

The next step is to pass the element of air into the wand. While holding the wand in your left hand, use the index finger of your right hand over the wand to trace the five-pointed star (see illustration on page 127), moving from the starting point and back again. In other words, trace the entire figure above the wand, passing the force of air into it. Do this three times. To enhance this technique, blow your breath across the wand each time prior to tracing the pentagram over it.

Next, pass the wand through the incense smoke, saying,

"Be you the summoner, the stirrer of mystical air."

Once this is completed, wrap the wand in a cloth and suspend it with a cord tied to a tree branch. Do this preferably on the night of a full moon. If circumstances prevent you from using a tree, then suspend the wand in your home somewhere (a temporary hook in the ceiling or door frame will serve nicely). Leave the wand suspended for the night. It is then ready to use.

To Charge by Fire

To charge by fire, light a red candle and some spicy incense, such as cinnamon. Pass the wand through the candle flame three times, saying,

"Through the transformational force of fire, I change this tool from a mere physical item into a magical implement."

The next step is to pass the element of fire into the wand. While holding the wand in your left hand, use the index finger of your right hand over the wand to trace the five-pointed star (see illustration on page 127), moving from the starting point and back again. In other words, trace the entire figure above the wand, passing the force of fire into it.

Next, hold the tip of the wand in front of your vision so that it blocks out the flame and you see the glow behind it from the candle. Slowly lower the wand so that the flame appears to sit upon the tip of the wand. You can experiment with closing one eye through which to view this effect.

Imagine the wand is a magical torch that can bear a flame or take one back into it. Move the wand up and down slowly to enhance this so that you see the flame appear and disappear. Once you can do this smoothly, repeat the process three times, saying these words:

> *"Wand, you bearer of the mystic flame, bring forth its force and draw it in again."*

The wand is now ready to use. In the meantime, wrap it in a red cloth or tie a red ribbon around it.

THE ATHAME

The use of a knife in ritual and magic is a very ancient practice. It is mentioned in pre-Christian literature and in books on magic and ritual over the following centuries. Traditionally, the blade is double-edged, and this symbolizes that it operates within material reality as well as nonmaterial reality. It is perhaps the most formidable tool at the practitioner's command.

The traditional athame has a black handle, which represents the procreative state of existence from which all things issue forth. It is black because black is the presence of all colors mixed together. This symbolizes the ability to open any single aspect with blackness. Black is also the color of the night, and in this way the athame is connected to spirits of the night. Among the four ritual tools the athame is the most "forceful" or "commanding" in nature, and it is used when this type of energy is needed in ritual or magic.

As a tool associated with the elements, some systems assign the athame to air and others to fire. This is similar to the view of the wand. As a tool of fire, the athame is aligned to transformation, and as a tool of air it is connected to the personal will (and the mind). In the case of the latter, the athame is the "sword of discernment" in the hands of the spiritual warrior, and it serves to cut away illusion. The athame has power, as a blade, in material reality and nonmaterial reality. Its mystical presence is just as powerful as its physical one.

On the material plane, the athame is never used for physical carving, cutting, or any mundane act. In its place the boline, a white-handled knife, is used. It is also the traditional blade used for harvesting herbs.

Charging the Athame

In an earlier chapter we noted a technique for magically charging the athame. Refer back to the material for the magnetic charge process. In this section I will present the alternative elemental charges for fire and air. Simply choose which element you feel the most connected to in terms of the athame, and then use the corresponding elemental charge.

To Charge by Air

To charge by air, light a blue candle and some incense with a flowery scent. Pass the athame through the flame three times, each time saying these words:

> *"Through the transformational force of fire, I change this tool from a mere physical item into a magical implement."*

Now, stand with your athame in your left hand. Then stretch both arms outward so that your body forms a cross (feet together and arms extended). Imagine yourself standing on the edge of a cliff and sense the feeling of a breeze blowing past you. Try to connect with this feeling of moving air brushing over you. This will establish a connection between you, the athame, and the element of air.

Now, point your athame into the imagined breeze. Blow your breath over the athame from handle to tip three times. Then quickly and firmly swing the blade back and forth. Try to create the sound of the blade whipping through the air.

The next step is to pass the element of air into the athame. While holding the athame in your left hand, use the index finger of your right hand over the blade to trace the five-pointed star, passing the force of air into it. Do this three times. To enhance this technique, blow your breath across the blade each time prior to tracing the pentagram over it.

Next, pass the athame through the incense smoke, saying,

> *"Be you the summoner, the stirrer of mystical air."*

Once this is completed, wrap it in a cloth and suspend it with a cord tied to a tree branch. Do this preferably on the night of a full moon. If circumstances prevent you from using a tree, then suspend the athame in your home somewhere (a temporary hook in the ceiling or door frame will serve nicely). Leave the athame suspended for the night. It is then ready to use.

To Charge by Fire

To charge by fire, light a red candle and some spicy incense, such as cinnamon. Pass the athame through the candle flame three times, saying:

> *"Through the transformational force of fire, I change this tool from a mere physical item into a magical implement."*

The next step is to pass the element of fire into the athame. While holding it in your left hand, use the index finger of your right hand to trace the five-pointed star over the athame, passing the force of fire into it.

Next, hold the tip of the athame in front of your vision so that it blocks out the flame and you see the glow behind it from the candle. Slowly lower the athame so that the flame appears to sit upon the tip of the athame. You can experiment with closing one eye through which to view this effect.

Imagine the athame to be a magical torch that can bear a flame or take one back into it. Move the blade up and down slowly to enhance this so that you see the flame appear and disappear. Once you can do this smoothly, repeat the process three times, saying these words:

> *"Athame, you bearer of the mystic flame, bring forth its force and draw it in again."*

Finish the charge by standing with your arms down by your sides with the athame in the right hand. In your mind, picture flames shooting up from a bonfire. Sense yourself as fire, and then quickly thrust both arms upward as though they are jetting flames (be careful with the blade). Repeat this three times.

The athame is now ready to use. In the meantime, wrap it in a red cloth or tie a red ribbon around it.

The Chalice

The chalice represents the element of water. Its history as a ritual tool goes back to its origins as a shell or gourd, or even a carved wooden bowl. In the beginning it was likely used more as a simple vessel, but later in time it took on mystical connections. However, it was the foundational associations from early periods that established the chalice as a sacred altar tool. Before looking at the chalice as a ritual tool object, it will be helpful to reveal its deep spiritual, mystical, and magical connections. These can be found in the myths and legends of the pre-Christian Europeans of the Old World.

The water collected from sacred and magical sites has always been regarded as having special qualities and virtues. The vessel used to transport and contain it is likewise given power through contact with the water. All this shares a relationship with the mythos of the Holy Grail, which before its arrogation by Christianity was part of the goddess cult of Old Europe.

The oldest vessels constructed by humans and associated with a goddess are the basket and the cauldron. This is a stage in the development in ritual objects that are intentionally crafted as opposed to being natural objects found in nature. In their design we find the incorporation of symbolism along with myths and legends being connected to them as cult objects. In the case of the chalice, we find the connection back to the cauldron, which itself shares a sacred mythos (as does the cup in the Grail stories).

The cauldron symbolizes the womb of the goddess, the vessel of generation and regeneration. It is the life-giver and the receiver of life returned to its origin. The cauldron appears in many tales. In myth and legend, it brews potions, aids in the casting of spells, produces abundance or decline, and is a holy vessel for offerings to the powers of the night, and to the Great Goddess. Its main attribute is that of transformation, whether of a spiritual or physical nature. As a symbol of the goddess it can bestow wisdom, knowledge, and inspiration.

One example is found in the tale of the cauldron of Cerridwen. The basic story recounts how Cerridwen prepared a brew in her cauldron that was designed to impart enlightenment to her son. The potion had to brew for a year and a day, which symbolizes the process of enlightenment. The story goes that a character called Gwion accidentally tasted the brew, which angered the goddess. She pursued the offender in a lengthy chase, and both Cerridwen and Gwion transformed into a series of various cult animals during the chase.

In legend, the cauldron of Cerridwen was warmed by the breath of nine maidens and produced an elixir that conferred inspiration. This seems to reflect the earlier Greek influence of the nine muses who gave inspiration to humans. It is noteworthy that in line 27 of the Taliesin riddle (from the Celtic work *The Tale of Taliesin*) we find the words "I have obtained the muse from the Cauldron of Caridwen." The muses freed mortals from the drudgery of physical reality and provided access to eternal truths.

In the Celtic legends Cerridwen's cauldron is depicted with a ring of pearls around its rim. It was located in the realm of Annwn (the Underworld) and, according to Taliesin's poem "The Spoils of Annwn," the fire beneath it was kindled by the breath of nine maidens, and oracle speech issued forth from it. This is similar in nature to the association of the Greek muses who were connected to the Oracle at Delphi. What is of interest to us here is the association of the cauldron in the Underworld. Cerridwen was a moon goddess in Celtic mythology, and yet her cauldron appears in Annwn under the title of the cauldron of Pwyll, the lord of Annwn. To understand this connection, we must now look at the Grail Mysteries.

In Taliesin's "The Spoils of Annwn," we encounter a group of adventurers who descend into Annwn to recover the missing cauldron. They locate it in Caer Sidi or Caer Pedryan, the legendary four-cornered castle. This is sometimes also known as Castle Spiral. In symbolism the spiral was, among other things, a tomb symbol representing death and renewal. It is here in the center of the spiral, itself within the center of the castle, that the adventurers find the cauldron of Cerridwen.

The tale is representative of many Mystery teachings. One aspect concerns itself with the Lunar Mysteries. Here the missing cauldron of Cerridwen represents the waning of the moon and its disappearance for three days (prior to the return of the crescent in the night sky). To the ancients, this was a time of dread, for the moon was gone. It had to be retrieved from the Underworld, into which the moon seemingly descended each night. The quest to retrieve the cauldron of Cerridwen is a quest to retrieve the light of the moon. The cauldron is the source of that light and belongs to the goddess. All of this can be extended to the chalice.

Examining the Chalice

As previously noted, the chalice is a tool connected with the goddess through womb symbolism. The prototype of the chalice was a gourd, a large shell, or a wooden bowl used to contain the sacred liquids of the rituals of pre-Christian European Paganism. By the Renaissance period at the very latest, we find the ritual chalice made of silver appearing in magical systems. Silver is a metal sacred to the moon goddess, and therefore in modern Witchcraft we typically employ this material for our chalices. Where once the wand was dipped into a wooden bowl or gourd within a ritual context, in modern times we often find the athame dipped into the chalice (wood to wood and metal to metal; like attracts like.)

Many ritualists employ a mortar and pestle, made of wood for ritual use instead of the athame and chalice. The word *pestle* is derived from the Latin *pistillum*. Pistillum is also the origin of the word *pistil,* which indicates the ovule-bearing organ of a flower. In this we see the connection between that which penetrates and that which is penetrated. The word *mortar* is derived from the Latin *mortarium* indicating both a bowl and a mixture. The etymology of the word *mortar* points toward a receptacle designed to be penetrated and mixed with other substances. In other words, the mortar and pestle are symbols of the procreative act of regeneration and transmutation.

In some rituals the chalice is used to hold the ritual wine. In matrifocal times, this was the blood of the goddess and the blood of the moon contained within the original gourd or bowl. With the rise of patriarchal power, and the creation of agrarian society, the blood of the goddess symbolized by red wine became the blood of the slain god of the harvest. The cult of Dionysus is perhaps the best-known example of such symbolism.

Within a spiritual context, the chalice is a vessel of offering and receptivity. Just as we, as worshippers of deity, are in effect vessels awaiting the pouring forth of spiritual light, so too is the chalice the vessel of containment and fulfillment. The chalice holds the intimate liquids of ritual celebration, just as we ourselves are filled with red liquid essence. In this concept we find affinity with the chalice, and in the relationship of being filled and emptied in our own existence. The chalice is not so much a tool representative of elemental water; the power of the chalice lies more in potentiality, what it can contain rather than what concept its material connects it to.

The Chalice in Modern Paganism

In the rites of such systems as Wicca, and related groups, the chalice is often used in a symbolic ritual called the Great Rite. Here it symbolizes the womb of the goddess, and in conjunction with the wand or athame it represents the harmonious union of opposites. In this light the chalice often appears in rituals associated with fertility.

The chalice is also used to contain wine for the rituals, and it is the cup from which libations are made to the earth and the moon. This involves dipping fingers into the wine and shaking off the liquid upward to the moon, and then pouring out a portion of wine on the earth. This act of reverence connects one in a spiritual sense to "above" and "below" and also serves to return the essence of the ritual back to its roots of power.

In some systems, the chalice is known as the witching cup and is passed around to participants within a ritual circle. It contains wine, or an herbal brew, and each member drinks a portion in a symbolic act of joining together in kinship. The chalice can contain a potion to induce altered states of consciousness, and each participant drinks some of it. This will later culminate in an astral or guided imagery journey.

In modern times the chalice is also used at handfasting or wedding ceremonies. Here it serves as the loving cup from which the couple drinks to symbolically join themselves together in an intimate bond.

The Chalice as an Elemental Tool

The chalice is traditionally made of silver, which connects it to the moon, and is associated with the element of water. The moon is the magical light of the Otherworld that shines upon a body of water such as the ocean, a lake, a pond, or even a well. To hold the chalice containing a liquid is to symbolically hold the essence of magic.

As a tool associated with water, the elemental tonal can be sounded over the chalice to awaken its connections to the life-giving and -dissolving properties. As noted earlier, the sound is the letter *O* stretched out with the breath—*Oooooo*. To enhance this, you use the elemental-invoking star, which is traced over the chalice.

One special use of the chalice is to bless, consecrate, imbue, or cleanse with the liquid contained within it. Objects can be dipped into the chalice or a portion of its contents can be poured out over something you want influenced or affected. Think in terms of what the water/wine represents and what you want to accomplish.

Just before using the liquid you can speak words such as "In the name of . . ." or "by the power of" to indicate the source that oversees the process. You should indicate what you are bringing about by using words such as "I bless" or "I consecrate" and then state the influence or effect desired. Here is an example:

> *"In the name of the goddess of the moon, I consecrate this object to be in her service."*

Here's another:

"I imbue this object with the dissolving force of water and remove all contamination."

The words are finalized with the action of pouring out the liquid or immersing the object in the chalice.

Consecration of the Chalice

Unlike the other ritual tools, the chalice is not "charged" per se, but is instead blessed, devoted, or consecrated (it does, however, contain charged fluids). Ideally, a blessing should be performed beneath the full moon. From a mystical perspective, this is best done when the moon is in the sign of Pisces, Cancer, or Scorpio. These are all water signs and are considered to be the most psychic signs of the zodiac (as well as being connected to anything fluid, whether frozen, steam, or liquid).

To begin, place a cup of water, a cup of wine, and your chalice on a work area outside beneath the moon. If something prevents this setting, you can make your work area near a window or on a balcony from which you can see the moon. Hold the chalice up to the moon and say:

"I dedicate this chalice to the moon, to the goddess of the moon, to the night, and to the deep mysteries concealed in the black depths of the outer space."

Set the chalice down and hold the cup of water up to the moon and say:

"With this water that represents the mystical essence of the moon, I imbue the chalice with this virtue and character. I pour into the chalice the timeless primordial waters blessed by the moon's light through the ages."

Pour the water into the chalice. Then hold the chalice up to the moon and say:

"Chalice, you are the bearer and container of the moon's mystical essence."

Next, rock the chalice back and forth to give motion to the water. (Don't be concerned about spilling.) As you do this, say:

"You wield the element of water."

Now pour the water back into the cup, and then hold the cup of wine up to the moon and say:

"With this wine that represents the sacred lifeblood of the mysteries, I imbue the chalice with the magic of birth, life, death, and rebirth."

Pour the wine into the chalice, hold the chalice up to the moon, and say:

"Chalice, you contain the wine of sacrament, the sacred lifeblood of the mysteries of birth, life, death, and rebirth."

(At this stage, you can verbally dedicate the chalice to the service of a particular goddess, if desired.)

Now, pour the wine back into the cup. Leave the chalice on your work area and take the cup of water and wine outside to a place where you can toss the liquids up toward the moon. Once you have done this, return to the work area. Clean the cups and the chalice and put them away.

Now that we have looked at the four elemental tools, let us turn briefly to a consideration of another force to which they connect. This is known as the forces of Od and Ob (the Odic forces). In previous books I have written extensively on this subject. In this section I will simply cover the basic concept.

In occult teachings there exists a concept known as the "magical universal agent." In its passive state it is known as Ob, and in its active state it is call Od. The agent itself is Aour when it reveals itself wholly in its equilibrated power. In symbolism these forces are illustrated in the form of a caduceus. This is comprised as an upright rod mounted with an orb on its top, with two entwined serpents climbing up the rod to the orb.

The rod represents the human spine, which itself contains neural pathways. The serpent on the left side (labeled Ob) represents the neural pathways of the left side. The serpent on the right side (labeled Od) represents the neural pathways of the right side. The orb on top represents enlightenment of the mind, harmony within the body, and evolution of the soul.

The use of serpent symbolism connects the concept of the magical universal agent with ancient thought. Serpents have long been regarded as chthonic beings of the Underworld. They also represent sexual energy as the vitalizing force of occult zones within the body. In particular, neural pathways join the nipples and genitals together as one flowing circuit, forming a downward triangle. Use of this current is highly effective in producing magical elixirs.

In old lore, serpents guard fruit-bearing trees, and sometimes in such tales they appear as dragons. The fruit they guard bestows enlightenment or immortality. Exceptional acts are required in order to obtain the fruit. In the case of the caduceus, it can be regarded as a tree bearing one single fruit, which is guarded by twin serpents. This reflects the mythical image of the moon tree, which bears one single white fruit. To taste of this fruit is to gain enlightenment and to undergo transformation. Before leaving this theme, it should be noted that serpents also guard the grain. Grain was one of the symbols of the Inner Mysteries in ancient cults, and is the core of the Rite of Cakes and Wine.

Returning to the caduceus symbol, the Ob serpent is passive/receptive. It is also shadowy, and is associated with chthonic elements, divination/oracle, and dream realms. The Od serpent is active/forceful. It is regenerative and is associated with worldly matters, outward energetic flows, and manifestations on the material plane.

When the serpents of Od and Ob are brought together in unity, they generate a state of consciousness known as Aour. It is the balance, the oneness of the conscious and subconscious, and is what results when electrical and magnetic forces (of an ethereal nature) join to become a third element.

Within the material world, Odic energy is what we perceive of as coming from all objects, the land and all its features. In some cultures this is not unlike the concept of *mana* or *prana*. The energy of Ob is what lies in the unmanifest. In quantum terms we can liken the Ob to the wave frequency, and the Od to the particle frequency. Likewise, we can say that the Ob is astral-like in nature and Od is the manifest nature—a thought that becomes a thing. In essence, this is more about the forces and the process than it is about the end results.

The famous occultist Eliphas Lévi (1810–1875) spoke of the Odic force as being a substance as indifferent to movement as it is to rest. He taught that nothing was truly at rest or in movement because one evoked the other and always resulted in an eventual state of equilibrium. Lévi said that a fixed nature attracts a volatile nature in order to fix it, and that volatile attracts fixed in order to volatize it. He often referred to the principle underlying this force as elementary matter. Essentially, one thing can only be defined by the existence of its opposite. In other words, to understand what is negative, one must understand what is positive.

Lévi taught that the Odic force, although not identifiable with the forces of electricity and magnetism of physics, is essentially the basis for the laws of physics as applied to such forces. The Odic force is present everywhere in time and space. In quantum mechanics we might say that something is everywhere at once, but at the same time can be more discernable at a specific point. So too is the nature of Od, and we can say that the Odic force is more concentrated in one thing than in another. For practical purposes we find the presence of this force most noted in stellar radiation, electromagnetic fields, chemical reactions, metabolic function, and crystal formations. All of these aspects can be found in the ancient arts of alchemy and Witchcraft.

THE ODIC BREATH

The energy described as Odic can be accumulated and condensed for magical purposes through deep breathing exercises or sexual stimulation. The resulting product can be passed into the blood by a technique known as informing, which is then employed for magical purposes. Informing is the act of passing one's desired goal into a generated energy-form, impregnating it with the desired manifestation. The basic technique is to raise an energy sphere between both hands, and then pass the desire from the mind through the breath, into the sphere. Imagine forming the sphere like packing a snowball. Imagine your words of desire floating out upon your breath into the sphere. The technique is very simple and can performed by following these basic steps:

1. Relax your body and allow your thoughts to become calm. Still the mind.

2. Focus your attention upon the desire of your magical spell. See its outcome clearly in your mind.

3. Rouse the emotions in order to charge the blood. Fill yourself with the desire for the outcome by deeply breathing in, working yourself up in the process. If employing sexual stimulation as a power source, begin during this phase.

4. With either method, begin deep breathing through the mouth only, taking in and releasing four breaths in succession while drawing in the stomach muscles slightly. This will keep air out of the stomach and help you to fill the lungs only.

5. Hold the breath on the next inhale and mentally transfer the image of your desire to the heart area/chakra.

6. Slowly release the breath out upon the object you wish to charge. As you do so, mentally transfer the image of the desire, seeing the image carried out upon the breath. Your desire is now magically transferred into the object and will vibrate with the energy of your desire (thus attracting it, like unto like).

CHAPTER SEVEN

THE AXIOMS

Love and Wisdom beget the spirit of truth, interior light; this light illuminates us and makes supernatural things objective to us.

—Karl von Eckartshausen, *The Cloud Upon the Sanctuary*

In Witchcraft we find axioms that help us understand metaphysical principles that might otherwise confuse or elude us. By strict definition an axiom is a statement that is taken to be true, and it serves as a premise or starting point for further reasoning, contemplation, and discussion. In this section we will look at the primary axioms.

In addition to the axioms, we will also examine ritual and magical concepts that are foundational to the inner mechanism of Witchcraft as a system.

THE LAW OF THREE

In popular views we find the teaching that whatever a person does returns to her or him with three times the intention. However, there is no parallel in physics to which we can point as an example. Typically, for every metaphysical concept the principle is also found in the laws of physics. For example, if you throw a rock up in the air, it does not come down three times faster than it went up. It comes down with the same amount of energy that sent it up.

In the Rooted Ways the view is that one action causes a ripple that affects us on three levels: mind, body, and spirit. For example, if we do an act of kindness for another person, we typically feel good about it. This brings an endocrine gland secretion that makes us feel happy, so our thoughts are uplifted and our body feels an inner warmth. This in turn lifts up the spirit, and so we have been temporarily transformed on a triple level by one action.

TO KNOW, TO WILL, TO DARE, TO BE SILENT

These are the words of the magical master.

To know something, we must do more than satisfy our curiosity; we must study not only the concept but also those things that relate to the concept.

To will, we must endure without yielding to defeat or discouragement; we must know our path and walk it despite its obstacles.

To dare, we must be willing to accept the risks of disfavor and mistreatment; we must be true to the path we walk whether the road is smooth or covered with pitfalls and jagged rocks.

To be silent, we must simply speak our truths without pretension of vanity. A Witch should never take on the role of victim; realize that you are a full participant in the state of your life. Be the Witch you profess to be.

A CHOSEN ONE OF THE SECRET FEW

In the late 1960s and early 1970s there was a teaching about the fellowship or society of the Witches. It was taught that Witchcraft was never intended to be a "religion for the masses" but was instead an inner or secret society.

It was said that Witches were chosen by the "Powers that Be" in each living generation. Souls were called to reincarnation in order to return among their own kind. They were to meet, remember, and know again those who previously held fellowship with them. This created either a blood lineage (being reborn into one's Witch family) or a spiritual lineage (a reincarnated Witch without past blood ties to the parents).

The occult principle is that with each reincarnation the Witch becomes more proficient in her or his powers of Witchery. This was thought to be particularly true of hereditary Witches within specific bloodlines.

It was fairly widespread back in the day for Witches to think of themselves as being part of a long-standing secret group. One found her or his way in or was called in some way, perhaps through some type of occult beacon. The latter gave rise to the idea of being "chosen" in some way. In this light, we were "chosen ones of the secret few"—not in any egoic or elitist way, but in an inner knowing way of one's place.

From many Book of Shadows texts during this period, the following poem was passed on. It is the words of the goddess to the recognized Witch:

My love is as endless as the skies,

As deep as all the seas,

As soft and gentle as summer rain

Falling softly through the trees.

My love is gentle, yet strong and true,

I can give it only to a chosen few.

My love is gentle as summer rain

Yet strong as the tempest wild.

It is pure and simple as the love of old,

Like the gods who are worshipped from time untold,

So, take this love I offer you

A chosen one of the secret few

This concept conveys the teaching that our ancestors passed on their experiences to us in the living generations. They, in effect, cleared the way for us through their practices, insights, and experience. In each generation we begin our walk where those who came before us left off. This is why it is called the Well-Worn Path, because it has been trod by the many.

When we begin our own walk as Witches, we clear and extend the path in front of us. The walk is ever ancient and ever new. Those who follow behind us benefit by where our feet have been and to where they lead the seeker.

IF IT HARM NONE, DO AS YOU WILL

This axiom promotes the idea that no one should be harmed by your thoughts, magical workings, or actions. It is an ideal. However, in nature harm is a daily part of obtaining food. Additionally, our bodies continually harm and destroy invading viruses and bacteria.

In human society we imprison people for crimes, and these people are put in harm's way in prison life. We also take away their freedom, their personal free will. So, we can see that "harm none" is a difficult position to maintain.

In the Rooted Ways we have only one law that relates to this basic theme. That law states that we never harm the innocent. Then we define innocent as one who does not provoke us. To provoke is to lose the protection of being innocent because you no longer are.

THE WITCHES' CREED

Author and Witch Doreen Valiente (1922–1999) popularized some Witchcraft tenets of belief in her poem "The Witches' Creed." In essence, it addresses the enchanted worldview of the Witch along with her or his participation in the ways of Old Witchery.

The creed presents us with the idea that we share existence with universal life. It speaks of the Witch's awareness drawn from secrets hidden in the night. Here she says that we come to know them through the quintessence (a theme we examined in chapter 1).

The creed points to a participation in the eight seasonal rites of Witchcraft, and through this the Witch is kept in the natural flow and cycles on nature. In the 1960s we referred to Witchcraft as a nature religion, and this seems to be what the creed is telling us.

In the creed we find an emphasis on the Otherworld nature of Witchcraft. The words of the creed say this of the ways:

This world has no right then to know it,

And world of beyond will tell naught.

The oldest of Gods are invoked there,

The Great Work of magic is wrought.

For two are the mystical pillars,

That stand at the gate of the shrine,

And two are the powers of nature,

The forms and the forces divine.

The dark and the light in succession,

The opposites each unto each,

Shown forth as a God and a Goddess:

Of this did our ancestors teach.[1]

"The Witches' Creed" teaches that the Divine can be separated into polarities. From this we can perceive of a goddess and a god who Witches can envision.

It is in "The Witches' Creed" that we find the passage of not harming anyone (or anything). Some Witches regard this as law, while others see it as a guide or something worthy of attainment in one's spiritual path.

IN THE NAME OF

It is very common to call upon the name of a deity, entity, or spirit. This is most often performed to enhance or fully empower an act of magic or a ritual. Is it enough to simply declare something in "the name of," or is more required? From a magical perspective, we need an active connection or alignment. We need to be connected in an intimate way with what we call upon. It needs to be aware of us, and we need to be aware of it, beyond a nodding acquaintance.

Calling upon the name of a deity, entity, or spirit is empowered by the relationship we have with it. If, for example, I am a priest serving a deity, to call upon its name manifests an immediate connection because of the relationship that was created between us. If I have no connection at all with a deity, then calling upon its name is likely to have little if any response. If a deity is just a name and image we know

---

1 Doreen Valiente, *Witchcraft for Tomorrow* (Blaine, WA: Phoenix Publishing, 1987), 172–174.

about from books we've read, then we don't actually have an interactive relationship. Why would a deity grant us something when we've not previously given anything to it ourselves?

One important thing to know is that the gods are not our servants, and they are not there to "jump through hoops" for us or to perform tricks at our request. The gods are there to companion us, and so we must be worthy companions. The gods guide us, and so we must be open to their input. It is best never to begin connecting to a deity by requesting something from it. It is best to establish an altar, give offerings, and request to connect with it. Veneration is the initial key. Once we have this in place, once the relationship is active, then we can say "In the name of . . ." with certainty of the deity's involvement.

AS MY WORD, SO MOTE IT BE

This axiom refers to the integrity and steadfastness of the Witch's word of honor. The axiom is spoken following a declaration connected to a work of magic of a ritual act. It is meant to confirm and solidify the intention or desire or the work being performed. To be effective, the Witch's word must have power.

In earlier periods of human culture, a person's word held great value. It was reliable. Giving one's word was assurance of the outcome. In mainstream society today, giving one's word has far less assurance and cannot be relied upon as it once was in a former period.

In the Rooted Ways there is a belief that the Witch is watched from another realm. Here a reputation is formed. The Watchers of that realm bear witness, and spirit beings are informed by what the Watchers know of the Witch's character and power. These things are foundational to how a Witch can influence and manifest in accord with the Witch's word.

If the Witch's word means little or nothing in the material world, nothing in her or his social order, then likewise it means the same in the Otherworld. This can, and most often does, make the spell or ritual fall flat. On the other hand, when it is known in all places and settings as holding true, then that power is acknowledged and honored.

It should be noted that giving one's word is not the same as saying "I will." For example, saying "I will be there Saturday" can be subject to interference or derailment under various circumstances. By contrast, saying "I give my word" is, in essence, saying that nothing will prevent the expressed outcome. This is the core of the Witch's axiom, "As my word, so mote it be."

AS MY WILL, SO MOTE IT BE

The will power of the Witch is an important element of the Arts of Witchery. The will must be honed in order for it to be effective. In spell casting the spoken intent of the work precedes the casting and is concluded with the words, "And as my will, so mote it be!" This is a declaration not only on the material plane but also in the realm of spirits. With these words the Witch is tying her or his will power to the spell.

In order for this to be effective, the will power of the Witch must be unwavering. Will power is linked to whether or not the Witch follows through with her or his goals. If the Witch typically sees things through to the end, then the will power is strong. If not, then the will power is weak in accord. You can see how declaring one's will power at the end of a spell is tied to success or failure.

One thing to bear in mind is that spirits are listening and watching. They know your abilities. If your will power is weak because you often do not follow through with things, then this undermines your magic as well. Therefore, in such a case it is best not to conclude a spell with the words, "and as my will, so mote it be!" You are in effect saying that as weak as my will is, so is the power of this spell. This is a waste of energy; and it's a waste of time for any spirits that assist your Witchcraft.

THOUGHTS ARE THINGS

An old teacher of mine once said, "It is as if the universe is listening and watching" when we speak and when we act. This teaching is about how the universe responds to energy. In doing so it does not reward or punish; it simply matches energy.

When we speak in negative terms such as "I can never afford . . ." or "I'll never have . . ." we inform the universal intelligence about us through such a communication. The universe assumes that this is what we want because this is what we focus on in our life. It doesn't judge; it simply gives us more of what we invest our mental and emotional energy in each day. Using this knowledge, we can change the "energy desire" of our communication by rephrasing: "Let me see how I can afford . . ." or "Let me discover how I can obtain/achieve . . ."

It is an ancient belief that thoughts can become things, which means that your mind has the ability to manifest your desires. This requires your mental concentration, the ability to visualize your belief, and the raising of energy through your emotional investment. See your desire in your mind, believe in its manifestation, and direct energy toward realizing it in your life. Formulating a ritual is one way in which you can direct and manifest beneficial things in your life.

The formulation and creation of rituals has long been a part of Old Witchery. Rituals are a means of attracting and transmitting energy designed to manifest that which we desire. Some rituals are performed in accord with celestial events and others with seasonal tides of the earth. Another design is a daily ritual or alignment through which you can empower yourself.

We live in a world that makes it seem like other people have unlimited power over us, and that we are subject to this in many ways. One example is government officials who pass laws that affect us even though our consent was bypassed in the process. Another example is feeling subjected to the dispassionate ways in which many corporations adversely affect our lives and well-being through their business practices.

While we can, at times, feel like a leaf blown about in the wind, there is a truth that we need to embrace. That truth is this: whatever created the universe also created us. We are, in essence, the offspring of the Source of All Things. This is no small matter. Within us is creative power of that which brought about our own creation. The spirit of the artist is within the artwork. Think about that and what it says about you.

Through a daily ritual or alignment exercise you can claim the indwelling power within you. You can raise this power and consciously direct it into your mind, body, and spirit. In this way your entire being resonates with the energy of the Source of All Things. You can use this alignment for protection, creativity, endurance, competition, and other things that can benefit any situation in which you find yourself.

PERSONAL EMPOWERMENT AND ALIGNMENTS

In this section you will find some methods of creating alignments that will draw power to you and from you. They connect you with forces that are greater than the isolated self.

The following alignment is designed to fill you with the magical creative powers of the four elements. For this working you will need the following:

- Scented oil or perfume/cologne that is your favored fragrance
- 3 red candles
- 1 stick of incense (wisteria, jasmine, or rose is favored)

To begin this work, think about what you to need to feel empowered in your life or current situation. Once that is clear, then begin the ritual as follows.

Stand facing east; light the candles and anoint yourself with the scented perfume. Then raise both arms upward and say:

> *"My being is mind, body, and spirit. I am from the Source of All Things. Though my form is of the earth, my race is of the stars."*

Next, stretch out your arms in the fashion of embracing someone, and say the following at each cardinal direction:

> *East: "By the creative force within me, I call upon elemental air to transmit my desire."*
>
> *South: "By the creative force within me, I call upon elemental fire to transform my desire into energy."*
>
> *West: "By the creative force within me, I call upon elemental water to give forward motion to my desire."*
>
> *North: "By the creative force within me, I call upon elemental earth to manifest my desire."*

At this phase, light the incense stick. Beginning at the east quarter, walk in a circle three times while waving the incense in a clockwise spiral. As you walk, say these words:

> *"I am born of the world but am not of this realm. I am the offspring of that which created all things. I wield the forces that move all tides and seasons. I encircle myself with the personal power that is my lineage from the Source of All Things."*

After the third round, go to each of the four quarters, clap your hands three times, and say:

East: "By air, and by Source, be it so!"

South: "By fire, and by Source, be it so!"

West: "By water, and by Source, be it so!"

North: "By earth, and by Source, be it so!

Sit for a few moments in front of the lighted candles. Verbalize what you feel empowered to accomplish. Then take in three deep breaths slowly and feel yourself being filled with personal power. To finish, snuff out the candles and incense. The scent you wear from the perfume will serve as a reminder of your empowerment throughout the day.

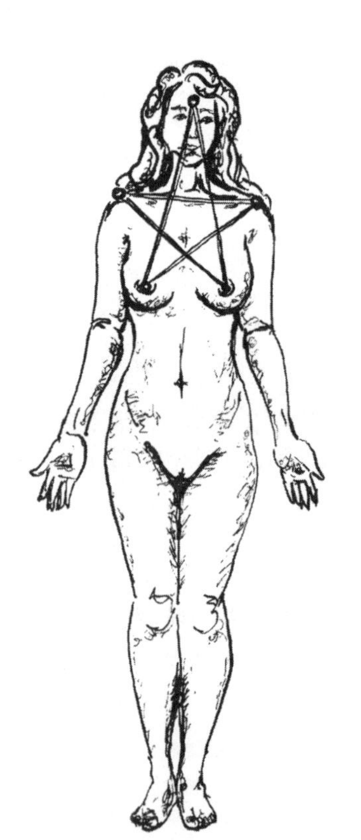

PROTECTIVE EMPOWERMENT RITE

For this simple rite you will need an oil of protection. You can make your own using a base of almond oil to which you add three rose thorns, a pinch of cinnamon, and three drops of lemon juice. Heat the mixture (do not boil) and then shake it thoroughly in a small jar or glass vial.

Anoint your body with an oil of protection, applied in this five-pointed star shape, to ward off unwanted energy.

Whenever you feel the need for protection, anoint your finger with the oil and trace a five-pointed star on your body as follows touching each position: forehead, right nipple, left shoulder, right shoulder, left nipple, forehead. After this, stretch out your arms and legs to form an X, and say:

"Strict charge and watch is given,

that to my mind, body, and spirit,

no ill intention may approach, nor enter in.

So be it done!"

DIVINE LIGHT ALIGNMENT

This is a simple alignment that brings you into a purified state and into a place of sacred space. Its goal is to fill and surround you with the light essence of the Divine Spirit.

Begin by standing with your arms stretched out to your sides with both palms facing up (you can also lie down). Take in a deep, cleansing breath and repeat these words:

"I am surrounded by the pure white light of the Divine Spirit.

Nothing but good can come to me;

Nothing but good can come from me."

Repeat these words three times in a row while visualizing white light gathering around you. Take deep breaths and envision white light pouring into you and filling your body from head to toe.

MOON "GRAIL" ALIGNMENT

This alignment is a spiritual connection to the sacredness of all that is associated with the moon and its powers in Witchcraft. It is best performed when you can see the full moon in the night sky.

Begin by pouring a small amount of wine into your chalice. Raise the chalice up to the moon, viewing it with only your left eye (the right eye is closed). Hold the chalice in a position where the moon sits slightly above the opening of the cup. Next, speak these words:

> *"Night Queen, Ancient Wanderer, Beloved One of the Ancestors, I bring you praise on this night.*
>
> *As it was from the time of the beginning, so it is now, so it shall be."*

Now, raise the chalice up until the moon disappears behind it. Imagine that the moon has descended into the chalice. Then say these words:

> *"Sacred light of the moon, celestial emanation of the sacred, now fills this witching cup."*

Close your eyes and lower the chalice in front of you (do not look back at the moon). With eyes still closed, say the following words and then drink from the chalice:

> *"I receive the divine emanation of the ancient light. I am illuminated within and without. I am moonlit and moon led."*

Remove yourself from the setting and do not look up at the moon. The idea is that the full moon is now inside you, so you do not want to see it in the night sky until another day.

CHAPTER EIGHT

THE POWERS THAT BE

For ye the circle's round we tread,
And unto ye the wine we pour;
The sacred Old Ones of this land,
Ye we invoke by ancient lore—

—DOREEN VALIENTE, "THE FULL MOON ESBAT RITE"

Some people regard Witchcraft as a practice, while others regard it as a religion or spiritual path. It is from this latter view that Witchcraft incudes deities, entities, and spirits. In this light we encounter the enchanted world of the Witch.

Our ancestors were at one time forest dwellers. It was there in that world that early ideas formulated about deities. Tree branches entwined above painted a picture of a boundary between the terrestrial and celestial worlds. Night and day presented different realities. In the time of sunlight, humans went about the daily life of survival. However, when night fell they entered a world of the veiled; they entered into a realm that gave way to dreaming.

In time the moon and sun became symbols for primal deities. In most cultures, but not all, the sun was assigned a masculine nature, and the moon was associated with feminine nature. The latter also included the menstrual cycles of women with the cycles of the moon.

In contemporary Witchcraft there appears to be an emphasis on the divine feminine. However, in the Rooted Ways the divine feminine and divine masculine are in balance. The former is assigned a celestial nature, and the latter is given a terrestrial nature. This provides us with a goddess and a god. In the Ash, Birch and Willow system the goddess is given the title She of the White Round, and the god is called He of the Deep Wooded Places.

Unlike people living in cities, the country or rustic people of the past focused on rural deities. These deities met their daily and seasonal needs. They had no need or use for an invisible deity ruling the vastness of the universe. For such people this was too abstract a notion, and such a deity was too distant from their lives.

For our ancestors, fertility was all-important and the deities connected to this were the ones most worthy of veneration. These deities were both terrestrial and celestial. It is here that we find, in Old Witchery, the Crescent-Crowned Goddess and the Antlered God of the Forest.

The eight seasonal rites of Old World Witchcraft include a mythos of the goddess and god. In this mythos we regard them as a mated pair who journey together through the year. They support each other and share reign. The god holds the equinoxes and solstices, and the goddess holds the festivals that fall in between. These are the "eve of" rites that fall on the nights before February 1, May 1, August 1, and November 1.

In the mythos of Old World Witchcraft, we find a similar but different tale of the goddess and god. On one level the story is the same; the goddess gives birth to the sun god on the winter solstice. They become consorts, and the god eventually dies in the harvest season. However, other older elements enrich the modern myth in the wheel of the year tale.

The primary difference between the two themes is that in the Old Ways the goddess is impregnated twice in the year. The first time is in May, and she gives birth to the bounty of nature in summer. The second time is November Eve, when she is impregnated by the god in the Underworld and gives birth to the new light (the new sun god). Therefore, we see "as above, so below" in which there is a spiritual impregnation and a material impregnation.

This Inner Mystery tale is embedded in the general mythos of the wheel of the year. Here the goddess is courted by the god in May. They marry in June. The god is later slain in the harvest field, and the goddess descends into the Underworld to reclaim him. From that union the new light of the year is born and the cycle of life is assured and renewed.

The beauty that lies in the mythos of the wheel of the year is that the story is also about us. It is the metaphorical tale of the mating of the soul and the body. In this we journey through the seasons of our incarnations. We share existence with the divine feminine and masculine within us. Ultimately, we become liberated from the wheel and we return to the Divine Spirit as educated and evolved souls.

THE CRESCENT-CROWNED GODDESS

As previously noted, the goddess is associated with the moon and its cycles. In this way she is the creator as seen in the appearance of a waxing crescent that grows into a full moon. She also integrates all things back into herself that she generates outward. This is presented by the waning of the moon (until it becomes unseen in the night sky).

The moon goddess is intimately connected to Witchcraft. Ancient writings reveal the theme of Witches calling upon her. One example is the Witch known as Medea who was depicted as a priestess of Hecate. Ancient writers such as Horace, Lucan, and Ovid paint the picture of a triformis goddess of Witchcraft who was comprised of Hecate, Diana, and Proserpina.

In Ovid's *Metamorphoses*, we find the Greek hero Jason swearing an oath to Medea, saying, "he swore by the rites of the threefold goddess and all the power which haunted that sacred wood."[1]

The goddess of the moon is intimately connected to Witchcraft and the Inner Mysteries of the human cycles connected with birth, life, death, and renewal.

The ancient writer Lucan speaks of the goddess Proserpina (but under her Greek name), saying, "Persephone, loathing sky and mother; and the lowest form of our [the witches'] Hecate, through whom the shades and I in silent utterance may commune . . ."[2]

Horace points to the goddess Diana in the *Epodes*. Here the Witch Canidia gives an incantation:

> *"O ye faithful witnesses to my proceedings, Night and Diana, who presidest over silence, when the secret rites are celebrated: now, now be present . . ."*

---

1 Ovid, *Metamorphoses*, trans. David Raeburn (New York: Penguin Books, 2004), 252.
2 Lucan, *Civil War,* trans. Susan H. Braund (New York: Oxford University Press, 2008), 125.

As seen in ancient themes, the goddess contains a triformis nature within herself, and in modern times she is regarded as the maiden, mother, and crone. These attributes connect with the phases of the moon: waxing (maiden), full (mother), and waning (crone). In the Rooted Ways she is seen as one goddess who can show one of her facets individually when called upon.

As a lunar goddess, she reveals the Inner Mysteries of the timeless cycles of life and death. In sacred imagery we see her in a grotto at the entrance to a cave. This represents the portal to the Underworld or Otherworld of myth and legend. Water trickles from the cave, symbolizing the mythical river of descent and ascent (that connects the Otherworld to the Mortal World).

She holds a torch that symbolizes the power of the moon goddess to bring enlightenment to the places of darkness. A serpent is coiled around her arm, representing the power of transformation. It is the shedding of the old for the new, which allows movement and passage between the worlds.

The goddess holds a spindle that represents the life patterns woven by the cycles over which she reigns. By her feet is a cauldron, which is the womb gate, the receiver of life and the vessel of rebirth. Her imagery depicts her as wearing one sandal, and her other foot is bare. This symbolizes that the goddess walks in both the material and spiritual realms. Her consciousness is conceptual and holistic.

Further imagery shows the goddess wearing a necklace of thirteen pearls, which represents the lunar cycle of the year. A triformis triangle is suspended from the necklace, which represents manifestation. A lunar crescent crown adorns the head of the goddess, which symbolizes her divine essence contained in the light of the moon. Vervain blossoms decorate her hair and represent her as the queen of the faeries. This flower has a long folkloric link to faeries.

From a deeper perspective, the goddess is beyond simply being a goddess of lunar nature. The white round of the moon reveals that she is the whole of existence. All things are contained within her. One example is to envision her as the year, and to then think of the months as being generated by her or from her.

In this vision we find the Antlered God as the part generated by the whole in time, space, and event. The eight seasonal rites of the wheel of the year mark his monthly presence and the passage of his journey.

The wheel of the year is, in essence, the story of the return of the part back into the whole. The whole cannot remain itself without its parts, and so the god is brought back to the goddess. In Old Witchery the shedding of antlers is a sign that the god releases his self-identity and therefore makes his way to being absorbed back into the whole (where his consciousness is integrated back into oneness with the whole).

In time the goddess will birth him (at the winter solstice) so that through his journey she absorbs his experience of the world she created. Through this she continually adjusts creation.

THE ANTLERED GOD

The mention of a "god of the Witches" in pre-Christian literature is seemingly absent (or lost to us over time). It is in remnants of Pagan ideas related to rustic gods that we find traces of the old god of the Witches. Working with this theme, the Antlered God appears.

In Old World Witchcraft the god is envisioned in the form as a stag (most often a white stag). Our ancestors took the stag on as a symbol of the protector and provider, as this was modeled after the stag's nature of leading and protecting the herd. Early human tribes used the deer for food and clothing. The antlers were made into primitive tools and weapons. The Antlered God was also a symbol of fertility. The combination of these aspects made the stag a powerful and important figure.

In his sacred imagery the Antlered God wears a crown of antlers that symbolize his connection to the tribe as a role model. They also connect him with the Spirit of the Land. His antlers appear similar to the branches of trees, and in this he is Lord of the Greenwood Realm.

In his continued mystical imagery we see a wolf pelt slung over his shoulders, which represents the waning forces of nature. A stag is at his side, symbolizing the waxing forces of nature. This is an older theme of the popular figures of the Oak King and Holly King. This theme demonstrates that the Antlered God possesses more than one aspect in his being.

The Antlered God, "god of the Witches."

In the ongoing imagery we see the Antlered God holding a harvest sickle, which represents sacrifice and the giving of seed to renew life. This reflects another of his aspects known as Lord of the Harvest. Here he carries a basket suspended from his shoulder, which is filled with the bounty of field and forest.

In the Inner Mysteries of the god the basket is both his cradle and his tomb. It is made of reeds, which are intimately connected to his mythology. In the Antlered God's relationship with the goddess, he is known in one aspect as the Lord of Reeds, and in accord she is the Lady of the Lake (a title given to her in the spring).

With this woodland god we find imagery of the sun filtering through tree branches, which represents vitality and the energizing forces that flow to him. Here in the woods we see the Antlered God standing in the forest, which symbolizes the primal connection and meeting place between the tribe and the Divine Source of All Things.

His continued imagery includes boots worn by the Antlered God that symbolize he walks fully in the Mortal World. Here we see the consciousness of the god as linear and materially focused.

It is important to understand that linking the god to the material realm does not diminish his divine nature. He is actually the living presence of the divine within material reality. He is generated by the whole of existence and becomes the part of existence within the mortal realm. The part continually returns to the whole and imparts its gathered knowledge and experience back into the whole of existence.

In the mythos of the Antlered God, he grows in power and self-awareness beginning at the end of December as he prepares to enter the new year. With the passing months he grows antlers, and in nature growth follows in keeping with him.

His courtship with the goddess begins his movement back toward the whole and away from his sole perception of self. In turn, this state of consciousness leads to the shedding of his antlers. He walks toward self-sacrifice as the wheel of the year unfolds before him.

THE HARVEST LORD

In other sections of this book we have touched on the concept of the Harvest Lord. He is an important concept in Witchcraft as a connection to nature, and specifically to the cycle of plant life. In the 1960s and 1970s, some systems used affirmations that can be seen as being tied to the plant realm. One example is, "By stem, bud, leaf, and flower!" Another is, "Flags, flax, fodder, and frig!"

At its core, the symbolism of the Harvest Lord (sometimes called the Slain God) is about the cycle of life in the plant realm. Here we find the cycle of the seed as it creates a plant that in turn creates new seeds. This ties directly into the Inner Mystery theme of birth, life, death, and renewal.

The journey of the Harvest Lord, from his winter solstice birth as the sun god to his death as a representation of the harvested field, is our own journey as a soul encased in material form. Our soul is a seed of light that is planted in a flesh body (much like a seed planted in the earth). With the onset of life within us that joins body and soul, we emerge in the spring of our incarnation. Like a tree, we grow, branch out from our foundation into the world, and bear the fruits of our labor. Here we stand in the summer of our existence. Over time, we come to the realization of what we have manifested in life. We can see what arose in the planting field of our time on earth. This is the autumn of our existence, and the bounty of what we planted is all around us. Following this season of our life comes the time of decline. We shed that which no longer serves us; we release that which needlessly draws upon our life force. This is the winter of our existence, and we move toward renewal in the spring.

There are two main symbols attached to the Harvest Lord. The first one is the sickle. Its crescent-like shape connects it to the moon. In the Ash, Birch and Willow tradition, at the time of harvest the moon goddess bears the title Lady of the Harvest. The god bears the title Lord of the Sheaf. This demonstrates the concept that the goddess is the whole (in this case the concept of harvest) and the god is the part (Lord of the Sheaf—the thing being harvested).

The second main symbol of the Harvest Lord is the pitchfork. The traditional pitchfork has three tines (although some pre-Christian pitchforks had two tines). One view of the pitchfork is that its three tines represent the Harvest Lord's connection to the sun, the earth, and the Underworld. The sun warms the seed, the earth covers it, and beneath the earth the seed awaits birth.

In the Old Craft of the 1960s, we symbolically viewed the pitchfork as the two horns of the god flanking a torch or candle in the center. We find this reflected in the classic image of the sabbatic goat that bears a torch or candle on the top of its head. One popular depiction of this imagery is Baphomet, a goat-like deity with legendary ties to the Knights Templar. However, Baphomet is not typically embraced as the god of Witchcraft or Witches.

The goat head candle symbolizes the light of the sabbatic goat that illuminates the veiled mystery of night.

In my view, the Goat-Horned God is an evolution from the Antlered God. I think of the Antlered God as representing a Witchcraft that is largely untamed, and the Goat-Horned God representing Witchcraft as a formalized system. What I mean by "formal" is the Witchcraft of prescribed rites, tenets, and established protocol. This may be too broad a brush to paint Witchcraft with, but it's a way of thinking about distinctions.

In human society the goat became part of the farming community. The goat is originally a woodland creature, and in ancient times was associated with the god Pan and with satyrs. In the evolution of the goat as a domesticated animal (now of the farm), it brings the Antlered One/Horned One into the agricultural community. It is here that the Spirit of the Forest becomes the Spirit of the Land in agrarian society. In turn, the Spirit of the Land becomes the Harvest Lord, who willingly sacrifices his life through the falling seeds that announce the coming death of the bearer.

This connection to the furrow and the seed, the planting and the harvesting, is an integral part of the Grain Mysteries. The Harvest Lord is the embodiment of the divine masculine presence within nature.

The sign of the Witch is linked to the Grain Mysteries in harvest symbolism. The circle signifies the goddess, who contains all components. The circle is also the full moon, a visual reflection of the whole. The triple tines represent the god (stylized as a stang), but they also symbolize the crossroads, which is the Path of the Witch.

In the sign of the Witch the circle represents the whole, and the triple tines represent the Path of the Witch.

The crossroads is the place of choosing (and in the sign symbolism the self-sacrifice of the Harvest Lord is noted as his willing path). The triple tines also speak to the goddess Hecate as the gatekeeper between the world of the living and that of the dead. In the sign of the Witch we can see her or him as one devoted to the mythos of the goddess and god of Witchcraft. We also see the Witch as the mystic at the sacred crossroads.

The earliest allegations against Witches in the Christian era included gathering at the crossroads to commune with the dead. Therefore, the sign of the Witch incorporates all of this symbolism and identifies her or him with the cycles of nature: birth, life, death, and renewal. This declares the Witch as one who walks the ancient path.

THE COVENANT BETWEEN THE HUNTER AND THE HUNTED

The Covenant is a very old teaching that is tied to the stag in the forest, which connects to the Antlered God mythos. In this the hunter promises to reanimate the slain stag who is killed in the hunt. Once the stag has died, the hunter dips an arrowhead into its blood. The arrow is then shot off into the woods with the belief that it will be born again on the spot where the arrow lands.

The stag is then taken to the village and its antlers are removed. The promise of the hunter is fulfilled in two ways. First, the antlers are worn as a crown during a celebratory dance. This is regarded as animating the dead stag. Following this, an antler tip is taken for the hunter to wear. In this way the stag symbolically walks again in the forest as the hunter continues his entering of the woods. Therefore, the essence of the spirit of the slain stag lives on again in the forest as promised in the Covenant.

It is interesting to note a possible connection to the theme of transformation and transition in the myth of Actaeon and Diana. In the common tale a hunter named Actaeon happens to come upon the goddess Diana as she bathes in the nude. Diana, who takes offense, transforms him into a stag. His own hunting dogs then turn on Actaeon and slay him. Hounds are sacred to Diana. Are we therefore seeing a deeper meaning in the slaying of Actaeon? Is this a sacrifice of the Antlered God, who has been overcome by the beauty of the full moon revealed to him in the deep wooded places?

THE LAME GOD

A very archaic form of the god of Witches is known as the Lame God. In folk tales we find him connected to the figure of the village blacksmith. The blacksmith works with fire and water to transform metal into tools and weapons. These elements, in turn, are intimately connected to lightning and rain in a thunderstorm. Here we can symbolically add the booming sound of thunder to the blacksmith's hammer hitting the anvil. Some people view the god Hephaestus (Vulcan in Roman mythology) as being associated with legends connected to the blacksmith.

In the old lore of this magical blacksmith we find that he is made lame by the villagers so that he cannot run away from the village: the Achilles tendon of his right leg is cut. This cripples the blacksmith, causing him to limp and slide his right leg behind him. The lame walk is an important symbol of his inner mystery.

At the old core of the tale, the way the blacksmith walks is a remnant of him being a stag figure from an older time. The stag walks awkwardly when he stands on two hooves (tied to tales of him trying to appear human). In the Christian era we find their devil figure depicted with the legs of a goat, satyr-like. Here we have the awkward walk component of the legend. Tales about him depict the devil walking with a cane or being mostly seated in a chair, which is noteworthy. This might be a connection to Pagan elements that became hidden within Christianity.

In the 1960s the Lame God was part of a magical ritual for putting fertility back into the soil. This was performed on the first day of spring, and then again just after the autumn equinox. In this ritual a person playing the role of the Lame God led a spiral dance with the celebrants. At the end of the ritual he would emerge from the center of the crowd and, no longer being lame, do a brief solo dance while holding an antler.

CHAPTER NINE

THE HEART OF THE OLD RITES

The fire was lit, and the Dancer would lead the men in a slow dance through the village. They carried sharp pointed sticks. One man was the wolf and he would lay a trail, followed by the Dancer and then the other men, weaving about the village and back to the village green. They did it to show them the inner and hidden boundaries, which were quite different from the other boundaries.

—Dolores Ashcroft Nowicki,
Village Craft Workshop at the Temple of Witchcraft, April 13, 2018

It is from the spirit or soul within us that the commonality of rituals, prayers, beliefs, and practices arises. It is a mistake to ignore or bypass a system because of cultural bias. This is because humans think and design in human ways. Therefore, it is wise to look at what resides in different cultures, meaning the rituals and practices outside of a single favored regional culture. It is wise to understand that each culture is a singular perspective. Each is but one shining facet cut upon the jewel of greater knowledge.

While there is nothing wrong with having pride in one's ancestry, it does not automatically follow that any specific ancestors knew all there was to know. The value in looking at other cultural expressions of Witchcraft is that they can provide expansive views and aid in a greater understanding.

One of the things I find great value in as I study various regions of Witchcraft is the commonality. I feel that the commonality is the oldest part; it is the roots beneath the surface. When we look at cultures that had no previous contact with each other, we find common elements. For example, we will find that the ritual components include singing, dancing, wearing certain types of dress, making symbols, and connecting with deities and spirits. These cultures will also possess myths and legends. Knowing this, and exploring this, will help you grow in your realization of Witchcraft as a whole.

In this chapter we will explore the basis for the old rites of witchery. There are many books that present rituals of various kinds and share many methods and techniques. However, few reveal the deep roots that empower them.

The Full Moon Rite is very common to the majority of Witchcraft systems. There are a variety of rites that offer different connections. In this chapter we will look at the old foundational elements. These take us back to sacredness.

On the surface, the Full Moon Rite might seem to be all about the goddess of Witchcraft. It is true that the rite is largely matrifocal; but the god plays an important role as well, which we will later examine in this section. For now, we will explore the sacred lunar elements.

The ritual I am using as a model comes from the 1970s (in its most recognizable form) and was at that time only available to initiates. While I am not at liberty to provide the entire ritual as it was, I will present the key elements within it for the purposes of this section.

The ritual begins with the stated purpose of those Witches in attendance:

> *"We gather on this sacred night of our queen beneath the full moon to adore her symbol, which she has placed among the stars. And so, we join together to give due worship unto the great goddess here in the night; for this is the appointed time for all Witches."*

In this text we find several noteworthy references. The idea of the moon goddess being the queen of Witches is not unlike the concept of the faery queen in old lore. It is interesting to note that nineteenth-century folklorist Charles Leland wrote about the goddess Diana being both a queen to the faeries and Witches alike.

Reference to the "appointed time" is made and this is linked to the night teachings we explored in chapter 1. The night and the full moon bring the Witch into sacredness as well as into an expanded understanding of her or his place in the grand design.

The ritual text goes on to say, "As it was in the time of our beginning, so is it now, so shall it be." This speaks to the old idea of lineage, meaning that Witchcraft is timeless and rooted. The Witch is devoted to keeping the Ways and passing them on to future generations.

A key element of the ritual focuses on the chalice (or witching cup). It is filled with red wine and set in the center of the ritual circle. Here it represents the essence, the very core of what we seek.

Attendees sit in a circle and begin to softly chant the name of the goddess while focusing on the chalice. As this resonance is building in energy, the priestess recites the following:

"Goddess of the moon,

think you, yet even for a moment,

upon we who gather in your name.

Beneath the sun do men toil,

and go about,

and attend to all worldly affairs.

But beneath the moon,

your children dream and awaken,

and draw their power.

Therefore, bless us, O' Great Lady,

and impart to us your mystic Light,

in which we find our powers."

It is here that we once again encounter the occult virtue of the moon and its light. To be bathed in moonlight is to unite with the "fount of light," and through this the Witch is joined with ancient origin. It also addresses the different mindsets that are associated with mundane and spiritual life. For the Witch, the emphasis is on the night and on the dreaming time, which is magical and transformative in nature.

The old Full Moon Rite culminates in the Sabbat feast, or Rite of Cakes and Wine, as it is sometimes called. This involves consuming small cakes or cookies that resemble the moon in shape and color. The wine is the lifeblood of the goddess (her essence) and the cakes represent the god (his substance) in his Grain Mysteries (the cycle of the Harvest Lord). To ingest the ritual meal is to receive enlightenment and to realize the divine nature within. Here we find the words, "May you come to know that within you which is of the eternal gods."

This theme is reflected in the Mystery text we noted earlier. In the following context it is spoken over the cakes and wine to bless them:

"Blessings upon this meal, which is as our own body. For without this, we would perish from this world. Blessings upon the grain, which as seed went into the earth, where deep secrets hide. And there did dance with the elements, and spring forth as flowered plant, concealing secrets strange. When you were in the ear of grain, spirits of the field came to cast their light upon you and aid you in your growth. Thus, through you we shall be touched by that

same race, and the mysteries hidden within you shall be obtained even unto the last of these grains."

The Full Moon Rite concludes with the teachings of the Ways. This is sometimes called the Charge of the Goddess and is viewed as divine instructions to the Witch in her or his spiritual and magical walk:

"Whenever you have need of anything, once in the month when the moon is full, then shall you come together at some deserted place, or where there are woods, and give worship to she who is queen of all Witches. Come all together inside a circle, and secrets that are as yet unknown shall be revealed. And your mind must be free and also your spirit, and as a sign that you are truly free, you shall be naked in your rites. And you shall rejoice, and sing, making music and love. For this is the essence of spirit, and a knowledge of joy.

"Be true to your own beliefs, and keep to the ways beyond all obstacles. For ours is the key to the mysteries and the cycle of rebirth, which opens the way to the womb of enlightenment. Your queen is the spirit of witches all, and this is joy and peace and harmony. In life does the queen of all witches reveal the knowledge of spirit. And from death does the queen deliver you to renewal.

"In honor of your queen make cakes of grain, wine, and honey. These shall you shape like the moon, and then partake of wine and cakes, all in her name. For she has sent to you the spirits of old and ensured that you be delivered from all bondage. For even though you are born into this world, your race is of the stars.

"Give offerings, all, to she who is our mother. For she is the beauty of the green earth, and the white moon among the stars, and the mystery which gives life, and always calls us to come together in her name.

"Let her worship be the ways within your heart, for all acts of love and pleasure are like rituals to the goddess. But to all who seek her, know that your seeking and yearning will reward you not, until you realize the secret. Because if that which you seek is not found within your inner self, you will never find it from without. For she has been with you since you entered into the ways, and she is that which awaits at your journey's end."

THE RITE OF UNION (THE GREAT RITE)

A special rite is performed during the full moon ritual (and in some of the Sabbats) that has very ancient roots. In its modern form the rite involves lowering the athame into the chalice, which is designed to symbolize sexual union. Through this ritual concept the divine feminine and masculine are joined together.

A primal model, and likely an older one, is the pairing of the antler and the gourd. In time this became the antler and the cup (or chalice). The antler represents the slain Lord of the Woods, and the gourd or cup represents the womb of the goddess into which all life returns.

Earlier in the book we noted the ritual that involved the blood of the stag and the wearing of his antlers. This ensured his continued life force, and the wearing of his antlers brought the person into unification with this aspect of the divine masculine. Through this the principle of rebirth was shared, and the person wearing the antlers aligned with the stag to be reborn as well after physical death.

In the old Witch lore about the Antlered God he is not surprisingly associated with the afterlife and the Underworld. In this guise he is the "Usher of the Dead" who herds souls from the Mortal World to the Spirit World (and back again).

In mystical imagery the souls are depicted as riding on his antlers or holding on to them as the Antlered God makes his journey. Here the god is seen as a great white stag as opposed to humanoid form.

Returning to the idea of the antlers and the cup, it is in the uniting of the two that the way of "crossing over" and "returning" is made available to the Witch. In ritual design an antler is dipped in red wine and then placed above the cup. Drops of wine are allowed to drip down into the cup. This is repeated three times. Afterward, the ritual attendees drink from the cup to merge with the covenant of birth, life, death, and renewal.

Some writers have touched upon the theme of the wild hunt and the Antlered God. Here it is said that the "verdant spirit of the forest" is associated with the hunt, and from this arises the connection to death. In this lie the seeds that link hunting with harvesting.

In the sacrament of the chalice and the antler, attendees drink from the cup to merge with the covenant of birth, life, death, and renewal.

THE GOD GRAIN MYSTERIES

It is in the old autumn tide ritual of the harvest that we find the Inner Mystery teachings of the grain. It is the mystical story of the seed and the seed bearer. It is our story as a soul within the mortal realm.

In this ritual the priest portrays the god and stands at the west quarter of the ritual circle. The priestess (taking on the role of the goddess) approaches him, and the sacred dialogue begins:

Goddess: "I have come in search of thee. Is this where I begin?"

God: "Begin to seek me out, and I shall become as small as a seed, so you may but pass me by."

Coven: "Then we shall split the rind, crack the grain, and break the pod."

God: "But I shall hide beneath the earth, and lay so still, that you may but pass me by."

Goddess: "Then I shall raise you up in praise, and place upon you a mantle of green."

God: "But I shall hide within the green, and cover myself, and you may but pass me by."

Coven: "Then we shall tear the husk and pull the root and thresh the chaff."

God: "But I shall scatter, and divide, and be so many, that you may but pass me by."

Coven: "Then we shall gather you in, and bind you whole, and make you one again."

In part, this relates to the idea of the cakes and wine Sabbat meal at the time of the full moon. Here all who partake are made one within the ritual circle, are joined as kindred souls linked to future lives. They are also joined together in the ancient covenant that oversees the cycle of reincarnation. For the Inner Mysteries are about birth, life, death, and renewal.

CHAPTER TEN

DIVINATION IN WITCHCRAFT

Very probably the Wicce (the Wise Ones) were the first clairvoyants. In those days when their role was a combination of priestess (or priest), healer, and citizen's advice bureau, their psychic faculties would have been put into multifarious uses in everyday life.

—Justine Glass, *Witchcraft, the Sixth Sense*

In Witchcraft we find several methods of foretelling the future. They include everything from tossing the bones to palmistry, runes, and Tarot and oracle cards. All of these are effective in the hands of a skilled practitioner of the Arts.

My personal view of divination is that it is the art of revealing the outcome of patterns forming in the astral realm. Nothing is "fated" per se, but there are major transitions and transformations that can be met at pivotal points in life. Some people who later became famous always felt they would be. Songwriter and performer Bob Dylan once said that he felt that way about himself, and he told the interviewer that becoming famous is all about knowing something about yourself that others do not.[1] I think there is much truth in that idea.

It is said in some circles that between incarnations the soul agrees to a "soul contract" in which it knows all about the life experiences of its next incarnation. I have never been comfortable with that idea. I think it is likely that the soul knows some general conditions, and it gets a glimpse of the overall view so that it understands the lessons to

---

1 Bob Dylan, interview by Ed Bradley, *60 Minutes*, CBS, December 5, 2014.

be learned in the coming lifetime. However, things can change because of the free will of other people. Therefore, nothing is set in stone.

In this light, foretelling the future is not about informing people of things they cannot change (as in the idea of fate). It is instead something like foretelling the weather. Prevailing patterns are looked at along with currents and cycles. If things continue as projected, then it all turns out as predicted. If something changes, the energy shifts or something intervenes, then the prediction fails to manifest.

To me, divination is about helping people to prepare for what is likely to happen. This helps them to take the proper steps to deal with that or change the verdict. Divination is not about telling someone that you have no power over your future because that has already been decided despite the fact that is your life to live.

The system presented in this chapter is based upon lunar cycles and how they affect us. It also includes the role of plant spirits as agents of the moon's communication through the Greenwood realm. Therefore, the system is called the Moon Garden Oracle. As we noted in chapter 1, the moon and the trees join together in mystical ways for Witches.

There are twenty-four images in the lunar-based system. I think of them as two sets. The first set is comprised of the full moon, the waxing crescent, the waning crescent, and the black moon. These are turned facedown to conceal them, and then one disk is intuitively turned upright as the reading begins. The image that appears will denote the prevailing energy of the reading:

- Full moon: strong position; empowerment
- Waxing crescent: new beginning and gain
- Waning crescent: decline and shedding
- Black moon: full potential; all is possible

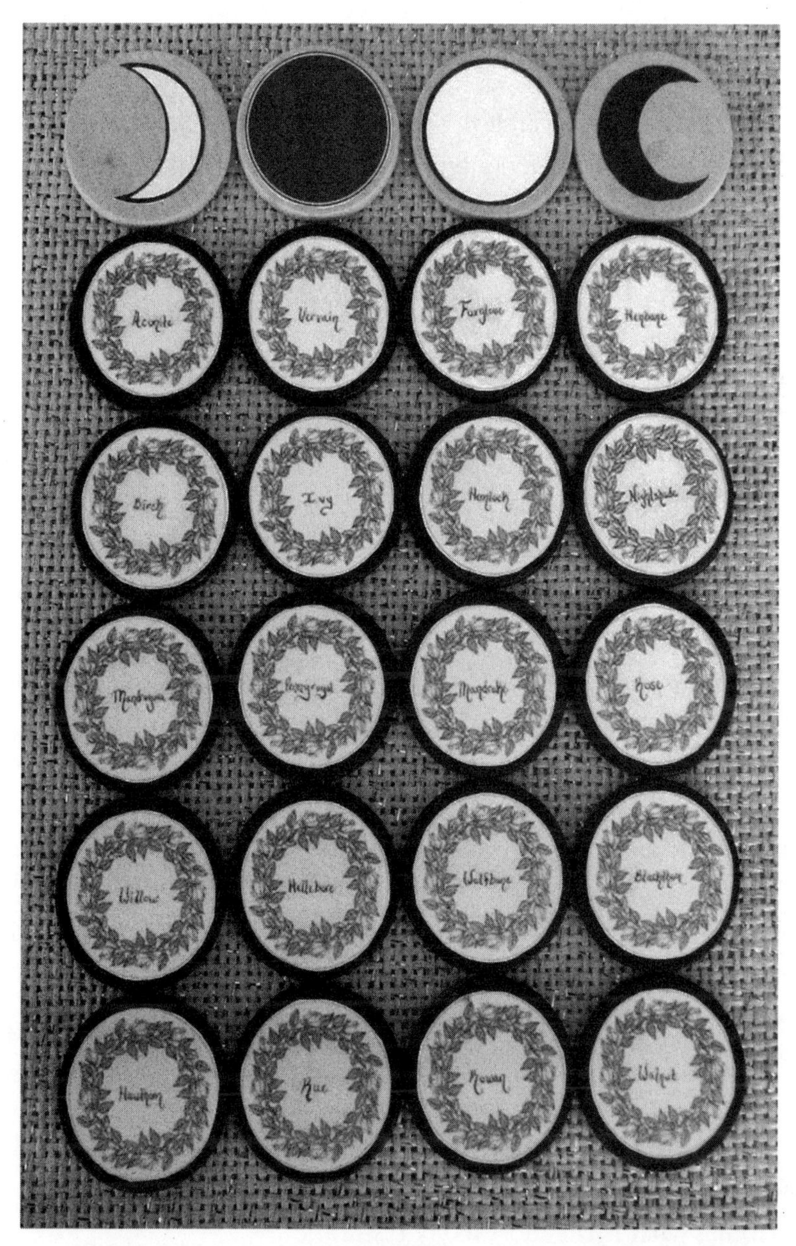

In the Moon Garden Oracle system, twenty-four disks are used to divine one's future: four list the moon stages, and twenty list various plants that signify different outcomes.

The reading then continues in context with the energy of the moon revealed by the moon disk.

For a general reading the remaining twenty disks, the second set, are either left in a bag from which the person getting the reading will draw, or all twenty disks can be placed facedown on the work area. In the case of the latter, the reader passes the palm of the left hand over the disks and senses which one to flip over.

The layout of the reading represents a mortar and pestle. There are four disks placed in a figure of a bowl (like a smile symbol). The three disks are set above the bowl, pointing down into it. This completes the image of a mortar and pestle set.

Moving from right to left, the first disk in the bowl setting represents the general influences. The second represents obstacles or challenges. The third is the foundation of the matter at hand. The forth represents where things appear to be headed at present.

Now we turn to the three disks above. The top disk symbolizes the role of divinity (what the divine brings to the matter). The second is the "outcome" marker. The third represents the option to the outcome. It may be supporting the outcome or it may show how to deal with it another way.

For reading on a "one question" matter, choose a moon disk, as you did for the general reading. This will set the tone for the insight into the question. Next, have the person getting the reading draw three disks from the bag. Lay them down (left to right) in a straight row.

The first disk represents the person in the matter, why things are the way they are. It is, in essence, the way the person feels (right or wrong). The second disk represents the heart of the matter, what needs to be considered and discerned. The third disk represents the outcome, what is the most likely result.

Once the disks are read and understood, draw one last disk from the bag. This disk reveals what can be done about the matter in question. It can also be looked at as further insight on what to do (or understand) based upon what was revealed by all three disks.

For a reading that asks for a simple yes or no question, use the two crescent moon disks. The waxing crescent will mean yes, and the waning crescent will mean no.

The reader secretly places one of the disks in each closed hand. Then he or she presents them to the person getting the reading, who will pick one of the hands. That hand is then opened to reveal the crescent and therefore the yes or no answer.

I always like to leave the person getting the reading with a "message" for them to take and meditate on. At the end of the original reading, lay all the disks facedown (including the moon disks). Ask the person to say out loud, "What do I need to know?"

Next, have the person slowly run their left hand (palm down) over the disks. Ask them to try to sense one of the disks, and flip that one faceup. Instruct on the meaning of the disk and invite the person to think about it over the next few days. It is, in effect, a message from the universe.

The meaning of each disk is interpreted in context with the meaning of its placement in the mortar and pestle arrangement. Additionally, view the layout in light of the phase of the moon disk that was turned upright. All of this will help you to better discern the matter of the reading.

MEANING OF THE DISK IMAGES

Aconite:	lasting memories, nothing is forgotten
Birch:	death or spirits of the dead
Blackthorn:	raw force and power to do what is needed; no limitations
Foxglove:	restore communication, open ways to reconnect
Hawthorn:	open doorways that seem closed
Hellebore:	calming of disturbances
Hemlock:	redemption from wrongdoing, setting things right
Henbane:	revealing the provoker, catching the offender
Ivy:	binding and holding in place
Mandrake (female):	conceptual view, spiritual perspective of the whole and the part interaction
Mandrake (male):	mediator, diplomacy; pay attention to details
Nightshade:	hidden secrets, revealing of secrets
Pennyroyal:	healing
Rose:	preserve oaths and confidences
Rowan:	protection from magic and spells; neutralizing force
Rue:	reversal of ill intentions
Vervain:	covenant with the Otherworld; working in common cause
Walnut:	the needed thing comes
Willow:	honor and integrity; taking the high ground; keeping one's word
Wolfbane:	banishment of the unwanted person, place, or thing

THE SKULL AND DIVINATION

In previous chapters we looked at ways in which the skull can be used for oracle messages. In this section we will look at scrying, which is reading the images that appear in a dark liquid that reveal the future.

To perform this, the reader uses hand passes over the liquid in a gentle circular movement. Passes with the left hand cause a magnetic energy to draw the vision. Passes with the right hand create an electrical energy that fine-tunes or focuses the vision. The reader works with both energies to bring about the visions.

To begin the oracle session, place a replica of a physical human skull on your work area. On top of the skull, set a red candle (to represent the flow of life's blood). In front of the skull, place two objects to represent crossbones (cross them one over the other to form an X). Using two white birch twigs is a good representation, as birch has long been associated with the dead. You can also find crossbones representations in shops during the Halloween season.

Place a medium-size bowl before the skull and crossbones. The liquid in the bowl must be dark. You can use a black bowl with water in it (for the effect) or you can pour a dark liquid into the bowl. I prefer the latter, and I like to use pomegranate juice, as this fruit has an ancient connection with the Underworld.

When all is ready, place a glass of red wine in front of the crossbones. Then slide them open, light the red candle, and say:

> *"Spirits of the dead, with this wine, remember life. With this skull, remember who you were. With these crossbones, remember how to move among the living. With these memories, regain the ability to speak once more. Let the dark waters bring forth a message of the future."*

To bring on the vision, look deeply into the bowl (not on the surface but deep into the liquid). If you need light, use a single candle and adjust its placement as works best. Let your mind be quiet; try to remain receptive. Don't force the vision. Instead, simply wait for it to form.

Use the hand passes to aid the vision to appear and focus. This method takes patience and continued practice, but in time you should be able to use it with relative ease.

Once the session is over, pour out the liquid on the earth. Close the crossbones and put out the candle flame. Leave them there overnight, and then put them away after sunrise. Sometimes the dead will communicate with you through dreams.

PALMISTRY

Among the oldest of the fortune-telling arts we find the practice of palmistry. Unique to this form of divination is the literally hands-on connection in the reading. The idea here is that the person's hands hold not only her or his life experience embedded in the lines on the palm, but also connect with future experiences that lie ahead.

A connective element here is associated with what some people call the soul contract, which is a metaphysical teaching about reincarnation. The basic idea is that prior to reincarnation a soul is provided with an overview of the next life and what lessons it can provide for the soul's spiritual evolution.

This energetic imprint is passed into the material body that the soul takes on as it forms within the material realm. Therefore, there is a "memory" within the flesh of things perceived from a higher level of the soul. In this light we can say that past, present, and future are reflected in the palms of the hand (for it is the hands that do the work of the individual in life).

Among the mystical elements of palmistry is what we call the Witch's mark. It is an X in the palm of the hand. Sometimes both palms will bear the X, which means that the person was a Witch in a previous life and is one again in this life. The right hand represents this life and the left hand symbolizes the past.

One element of palmistry involves the ability to receive impressions and information from various objects. This is called psychometry. Someone with this skill (or gift) touches an item with her or his hands. Through this contact the person can sense a variety of things. Naturally, this is of a psychic nature.

The lines in the hands fall into categories mapped out on the palm of the hand. This is much like laying out Tarot cards in a divinatory pattern. Each placement section means something, and the card is interpreted within the context of where it is set. It is basically the same with palmistry inasmuch as areas of the palm correspond to specific meanings. The lines of the hands are then read in keeping with the meaning of the zone on the palm of the hand.

Unfortunately, there isn't room to fully present the art of palmistry here. However, you can easily find a variety of books on the subject. I recommend that you try working with this method of divination.

OLD-FASHIONED FORTUNE-TELLING

The techniques in this section have very old roots and were once popular in the parlor games of the Victorian age. Although being very simple, they bring with them a cresting wave from the momentum of the past.

Card Divination

Using a simple deck of playing cards (used only for divination purposes), you can quickly divine your future and gain insight into your situation.

At midnight light a single candle in a dark room. Have with you four playing cards: the ace of spades, the ace of hearts, the ace of clubs, and the ace of diamonds. Holding them together, look at the candle and ask your question about your future. Then say the following:

"Candle here that burns so bright,

Reveal my answer now on this night.

Let the card reveal what I need to know,

The face of it the truth to show."

Now toss the cards up in the air and blow out the candle at the same time. In the dark, search for a card. When you have it, turn on the lights and see which one you found. Apply the meaning of the card to your question. Think about how it answers the question you asked.

Ace of spades: misfortune, not going to happen, wasted time and energy

Ace of hearts: love, friendship, good relationships, winning your desire

Ace of clubs: good opportunity, open doors, successful endeavor

Ace of diamonds: prosperity, great exchange, good fortune

Fire Spirit Divination

This divination method is perfect for a small group, but can accommodate up to thirteen people. Use it when you want to manifest something good for the future.

Take a medium-size metal pot on your work area. Write up thirteen individual fortune verses on thirteen pieces of paper. Securely wrap them in tinfoil and place them in the pot.

Pour some brandy into the pot and light it with a match. Each person in attendance will then sprinkle a pinch of salt into the bowl (careful to not burn one's fingers).

Next, these words are spoken over the flame:

"Spirit of the flame, now reveal, now show

What is it that I should know?"

Each person will then retrieve one of the wrapped messages using a pair of tongs. Allow the foil to cool, and then open and read your message.

WALNUT SHELL DIVINATION

This method is useful for when you want to have a wish granted. It can work for one person or many.

Make a wish. Then take two open walnut shell halves and half fill them with wax. Place them in a large bowl of water at opposite ends. Gently push them toward the center of the bowl. If the shells touch each other, your wish will be granted. If they do not touch, your wish is in vain. If after they come to rest they seem to hover near each other, this means there is another chance for you to gain your wish.

CAULDRON DIVINATION

Drawing one's fortune from a cauldron was a favorite method on November Eve. Practice this with a group.

To use this method, take four times the amount of paper slips than there are people in attendance. Write potential fortunes (good and bad) along with some slips that say: Yes, No, Maybe, and No Choice.

Drop the folded pieces of paper into a sizable cauldron.

One at a time, each guest asks a question, either out loud or silently to oneself, and reaches in the cauldron to choose a piece of paper and reads it out loud or silently. This would be a personal choice.

Tokens could also be placed in the cauldron to represent something, and the person may draw one of those instead of a paper slip. Here are a few examples of possible tokens:

- Ring: a loving mate
- Coin: money coming in

- Key: new opportunities arriving
- Lucky charm: good fortune
- Feather: an important message coming soon
- Thimble: protection in one's endeavors
- Small crystal: empowerment
- Small stone: stability, foundation, or endurance
- Paperclip: a successful conclusion to a matter
- Caduceus: good health or healing

These are just a few of the examples of divination. There are many more to be explored.

CHAPTER ELEVEN

THE PATH OF THE WITCH

[W]e have not even to risk the adventure alone; for the heroes of all time have gone before us; the labyrinth is thoroughly known; we have only to follow the thread of the hero-path. And where we had thought to find an abomination, we shall find a god; where we had thought to slay another, we shall slay ourselves; where we had thought to travel outward, we shall come to the center of our own existence; where we had thought to be alone, we shall be with all the world.

—JOSEPH CAMPBELL, *THE HERO WITH A THOUSAND FACES*

The world of the Witch is given light by the moon, adorned by the stars, and nestled in the embrace of night. Moonlit paths lead to the deep wooded places where the memories of ancient rites are whispered by the old trees that still reign. A new generation of saplings learns from the old wood of the forest.

Today the Witch still moves through the mystical mist of something primal and rooted. In this she or he is connected to the elder faith of our ancestors. The Witch finds wholeness amidst the seemingly fragmented memories of those who came before. In life after life the Witch returns to persevere, and to further pursue her or his journey through the enchanted world. Mind, body, and spirit are initiated through the rite of rebirth, and the Witch remembers.

Through the years the Witch walks barefoot through the organic memory of the earth and learns to reach upward to draw from celestial guidance.

In an old woodcut image from the Witch trial period we find an interesting scene. It depicts an initiation showing a Witch kneeling, with one hand on top of her head and the other under her foot. The description informs us that she is offering her entire self to the process. In essence, the image is saying, "All that is between my hands, I devote to the ways of Witchcraft."

The theme of the Witch as a vessel appears in various forms. Central to all of them is the idea of transforming the self in some manner. When we look at Witchcraft as a spiritual or mystical path, the idea of transformation is an inner one. One example of this is the partaking of symbolic cakes and wine in the Full Moon Rite.

In contemporary Witchcraft there are three types of commitment to Witchcraft as one's personally chosen path. The first is through being formally initiated by others. The second is through what is called "self-initiation" into the Craft, which is very popular today among solitary practitioners. The third method is a rite of personal dedication.

Charles Leland once wrote that a person can become a Witch through a serious study of Witchcraft. He also noted that this can happen if a person keeps company with Witches. Additionally, Leland wrote that a person can become a Witch through formal initiation. There is no direct mention of self-initiation in any of his writings. However, that being said, he does give us a simple tale of evocation through which a person may gain the favor of the goddess Diana, who, as previously noted, is a goddess of Witchcraft.

The gaining of favor, in Leland's accounts, begins by going out beneath the full moon, taking with you a red wool bag, some salt, a sprig of rue, and some red wine. These are laid out upon the ground, and then an evocation is spoken to Diana. She is asked to accept the speaker, and if the goddess does so, a sign of her favor is further requested. This sign is to be delivered through the sounds of various creatures such as the croaking of a frog/toad, the call of an owl, the barking of a dog, and so on. It is noteworthy that these creatures all belong to Diana's cult animal list.

What all methods share in common is a demonstration of devotion. It is a willful act, a declaration of heartfelt intent. This is required because the gods operate in an "action and reaction" energy relationship with us. Your actions cause ripples, and these ripples reach the gods. In turn, the gods respond back along the energy trail. The Otherworld also receives the ripple, and various entities and spirits notice you. However, is "favor" assured just for the asking?

In chapter 1 we looked at the idea of recognition and acknowledgment. We noted that the word *recognize* means "to know again" and that the word *acknowledge* means "to accept or admit the existence or truth of something." Additionally, we saw that the inner resonance of the Witch acts like a beacon. What the gods see is what they respond to; it is what they acknowledge or do not, and it is what they recognize in us or do not see at all.

We must be careful not to regard any of this as judgment. It is, instead, a matter of discernment. An important fact to remember is that this is not about being unworthy. The gods work with human flaws all the time, and a flawed vessel is not discarded. The true matter at hand is always about resonance, or what in the new age is seen as the energy of the aura.

The aura can be regarded as the star body of the individual. It is a collection of different energy emanations or manifestations. These energies are a blend of the resonance of the soul, along with the imprints of the human persona within the energy field.

The aura reflects the highest vibration that the combination of soul/spirit and human state of being can generate. In this regard we can call the aura the star shine of the individual. Stars shine in the center of the black night sky, just as our souls/spirits shine from within the center of our material bodies.

THE WITCH AS SPIRITUAL WARRIOR

In an old occult teaching the Witch is seen as a spiritual warrior. She or he carries the stylized weapons of the knight. These are the four elemental tools of Western occultism: pentacle, wand, sword, and chalice.

The pentacle is the shield of the warrior. Here it is called the Shield of Valor, because personal valor protects the Witch from all ill intentions sent to her or him. To be true to one's self is a powerful shield to carry in life. The Shield of Valor proclaims where we stand and what we do not compromise on in our lives.

The wand is the Lance of Intuition that alerts the Witch to what lies ahead. This is the psychic nature of the Witch. With the Lance of Intuition, the Witch can traverse the Path wisely, charting the route as things unfold.

The athame is the Sword of Discernment. This is the double-edged blade of the Witch that cuts through illusion and deception. As the athame is a balanced knife, so too is the Witch a balanced practitioner of the Arts of Witchery. Here the Witch works equally with the mundane and the magical worlds.

The chalice is the Helmet of Compassion. This maintains the receptivity of the consciousness of other people that the Witch encounters in life. This is the ability to see past the behavior of people and to look into their souls. The Witch, as a spiritual warrior, does not excuse or overlook ill and harmful behavior. Instead, the Witch notes it and remembers it for future dealings. However, the Helmet of Compassion bestows upon the Witch the ability to search for something redeeming in other people. In the final analysis, it is still a helmet of protection in the spiritual battle.

The "battle cry" of the Witch as a spiritual warrior is carried in this proclamation:

I am Pharmakeute,

I am the knower of plants,

Seer of all that approaches,

Hearer of the whispering dead.

I am born of this world but am not of this realm.

And I wield the forces that move all tides and seasons.

This addresses the five Arts of Witchcraft that are worthy of mastering in one's training: working with plant spirits, divination, magic, mysticism, and spirits of the dead.

THE WITCH AS SPIRITUAL BOTANIST

The Witch has long been associated with plants that are used in magic and the casting of spells. However, there is an ancient connection to the indwelling spirit of a plant. Just as humans believe they are souls encased in material bodies, Witches know that plants also have an indwelling spirit.

As noted earlier, the oldest word for Witch in Western culture is the Greek word *Pharmakis*, which evolved into the title of *Pharmakeute*. In essence, this is the Witch as one with intimate knowledge of plants, which includes their spiritual or mystical nature. In this we find the declaration of the Witch: "I am the knower of plants." This "knowing" penetrates all three levels: body, consciousness, and spirit.

For the Pharmakeute, plants are allies in the magical world. They network beneath the land and connect all things associated with that realm. Because plants are literally rooted in the organic memory of the earth, they can convey information to the Witch. This is tied into the fact that soil is a crystalline formation in terms of its minerals. Crystals naturally hold energy and can be used to direct it.

The classic image of the Witch stirring plants into her cauldron brew reflects the idea of the alchemy involved in plant magic. Here the Witch's brew of transformation is blended in accord with the Old Magic: "By seed, crown, stem, leaf, bud, and flower!"

THE WITCH AS SEER

Ancient tales of the Witch reveal a very old relationship between spirits and Witches. This comes through the ability of the Witch to perceive the Otherworld. By merging the Otherworld with the Mortal World, the Witch can foresee future events that are taking shape from the present.

Seership is very much rooted in the psychic nature of the Witch. That intrinsic virtue of the Witch allows her or him to connect to things unseen by the general populace. Knowing what lies ahead in the forming patterns is a sign of the Witch's intimate connection to the inner and outer worlds.

It is in the perception of the cycles of nature, the natural and supernatural emanation, that the Witch proclaims, "I am the seer of all that approaches."

A Witch serves the needs of her or his community by being available to perform divination for its members. This is a necessary skill for the Witch to possess.

THE WITCH AS MAGICIAN

Magic has been part of Witchcraft for countless centuries. The Witch is a weaver and shaper of energy that is used in spell casting, magical work, and rituals. The Art of Magic is central to Witchcraft as a whole.

There are essentially two types of magical energy: "raised magic" and "drawn magic." (All variants of magic can be assigned to one of these two.) Raised magic is the art of summoning up the personal power of the Witch. It comes from within and is proportionate to the time and practice that the Witch has devoted to the Arts. Drawn magic comes from an outside source. This can be from a spirit, a deity, an entity, or an event—or even from an object, such as a stone or crystal.

In some cases, both types of energy are used together. One example is the charging of a talisman or amulet. Here the personal power of the Witch imbues the charm, which in turn is connected to something outside of the Witch. Symbols link the charm item to, say, a spirit. The spirit is bridged to it while at the same time the inherent power of the Witch energizes it with magical intention.

In the alignment of the Witch to celestial and terrestrial forces, he or she is continually bathed in the magical essence. It is through this, and the connection to the energies of the earth's cycles, that the Witch can proclaim: "I wield the forces that move all tides and seasons."

THE WITCH AS SPIRIT MEDIUM

Among the earliest depictions of the Witch we find references to communicating with the dead. In ancient literature the Witch knows where the entrance is to the Underworld. The Witch also possesses certain knowledge about the dead and how best to communicate with departed spirits.

In one story a Witch instructs a band of Greek heroes on how to receive information from the Dead. She tells them to cut their palms and put some drops of blood into a cup of wine, which is then to be offered to the Dead. She goes on to say, "When the dead taste the blood they will remember life, and when they remember life they will recall who they were in life. And when they remember this they will be able to speak." It is in this light that the Witch can proclaim, "I am the hearer of the whispering dead."

For connecting with the dead, the Witch uses various methods and objects. In my personal practice I have used a sprig of cypress, as this is the classic tree planted in a cemetery. I have also used a cutting from a rosemary bush, as it has a long-standing connection to memory. Additionally, I still use a representation of a human skull as a link to the Otherworld.

In keeping with classic traditional Witchcraft themes, the Witch serves to convey messages from the dead to the living. This is often performed while holding a skull as an oracle tool. To aid in this the Witch can wear a pouch containing graveyard dirt and a piece of bark from the largest tree on site. This all contributes to the proper state of mind for the Witch to then become a voice for the dead.

THE WITCH AS MYSTIC

Among the things that set the Witch apart from others is her or his mystical vision. The Witch sees past the surface, past the manifest, and looks upon what lies unseen. The unseen is what projects the image.

One example is that when a Witch looks upon a forest, she or he sees a gathering of living beings. When a Witch looks upon the moon, what is seen is an orb of magical light in the night sky. This is the magical sight of the Witch, and it is shared in common with all the beings of the enchanted world.

There is an inner knowing within the Witch that she or he is different from non-Witches. This was a feeling when the Witch was very young, and it grew over the years into a knowing. This is because the mind, spirit, and body of the Witch are aligned to things that are much greater than mundane material reality.

It is the mystic nature of the Witch that allows her or him to see signs and omens. This is because the mystic knows that communication flows from all conscious beings in all realms. The Witch opens to that reality and thereby becomes a receiver.

The Witch recognizes that while she or he resides in human form, the greater being within is from a different world beyond this one. It is in this awareness that the Witch proclaims, "Although I am born of this world, I am not of this realm."

THE WITCH AS ROOT TENDER

One of things that distinguishes Witchcraft from folk magic is intentional preservation. In other words, the Witch strives to keep things intact, to preserve methods and techniques, recipes, and so on. This is not as prevalent among modern Witches, but in my opinion it is still an important thing to do.

By contrast, folk magic changes over time, as no one is safeguarding against it shifting and transmuting. Folk magic is typically modified, customized, and added to in order to suit the desire and mindset of the practitioner. It continues to bear a resemblance to its rooted forms in the past, but foundational elements often go missing over the passage of time.

As mentioned earlier, I often think of the Craft as a great old tree. Its roots are the oldest part but are largely unseen because of their depth. The roots provide nutrition to the tree and hold it in place against the winds of adversity. If it were not for this, the tree would wither away in time and topple over. We would lose the tree.

The trunk of the tree declares its presence and place in the world. It stands, and it has a position. It is recognizable because it looks like its kind have always looked (and in this we have something reliable). In this light, the Craft is the old tree that one can easily identify amidst all the other trees.

The new branches, flowers, and fruit represent the new practitioners and systems that arise. They are essential for the tree to continue to thrive into the future. However, in nature new growth arises from the old wood, and the old wood grew from what was provided by the roots. So, it is important to have people who tend to the new growth and who pick the new fruit. However, there must always be those who tend the roots. We all have our place and our purpose. Together we benefit from the blessings of the sacred tree.

The role of the root tender is reflected in the old concept of the Book of Shadows. This book was traditionally hand-copied word for word from an older copy belonging to a teacher/initiator. No additions, omissions, or changes were allowed. This ensured that the material was passed on intact, and that everyone down the line was literally on the same page, so to speak.

So yes, back in the day we hand-copied from our teacher's own book. This method allowed the material to be mentally absorbed through a mechanical method. There was energy in the teacher's hand-copied book; it permeated the pages. This brought to the process something magical. We touched the handwriting of one who had touched the handwriting of another, and on it went back down the line of its lineage. We were drawn into something greater than ourselves, and we became part of the Old Magic.

It is the role of the root tender to preserve the flow of what comes from a lineage. It is a sacred office to be the bearer of something passed on due to its integrity and power. In this light, the Witch is a steward of that which is sacred. It is why ancient groves had a specific sacred tree in them, and why priestesses and priests safeguarded and presided over the prescribed rites.

In keeping with the theme of the tree, the following is something I wrote many years ago, and I present here in a slightly revised form. It is called the teachings of the tree, a spiritual guide for living life:

The Teachings of the Tree

1. Have a position with deep roots in your understanding of it, and stand firm in your place within the world.
2. Reach upward to touch lofty things, and branch outward to extend yourself to the world.
3. Provide shade for those who need rest, and shelter for those who come to you.
4. Bear fruit and be abundant.
5. In the winters of your life, conserve your resources.
6. In your springs, take advantage of the opportunities for new growth.
7. In your summers, expand, thrive, and reach new heights.
8. In your falls, release what no longer serves, make preparations, and await renewal.
9. When all is said and done, leave behind some seeds.

THE WITCH AS PRIESTESS OR PRIEST

Those Witches who embrace the idea of Witchcraft as a religion often take on the role of a priestess or priest. As noted in chapter 1, ancient writing depicts the Witch Medea as a priestess of the goddess Hecate. Medea uses an altar and calls upon her goddess. This basic model is still with us today.

The role of a priestess or priest moves the Witch from being a simple practitioner to being in a refined partnership with deity. It is a special relationship in which the Witch offers formal veneration as a part of her of his life as a Witch.

It is common for the Witch, as a priestess/priest, to be a ritual facilitator and a counselor to other Witches in her or his circle. In this role the Witch performs weddings, child blessings, and funeral rites.

In the Rooted Ways the Witch, as a priestess/priest, will keep and maintain an altar. She or he will set up routines for venerations, often choosing Monday (moon day) or Sunday (sun day) as the specific time for altar work and meditation. This helps establish a deeper rapport with deity, which serves to strengthen the active connection to one's deities. Deity statues on the altar are cleaned as part of the veneration.

An important element of priestess or priest work is to study the Inner Mysteries connected to deity. This includes teachings linked to the sun, moon, stars, cycles, and seasons of the earth. This provides a deeper understanding of the gods and how we can interface with them through the mysteries they possess.

The office or role of the Witch is rooted in having a position that stands for sacredness. In this way the Witch serves a higher purpose. Here she or he is focused on being a channel for access to the Inner Mysteries. This role may well vary from Witch to Witch. What is important is where, how, and in what way the Witch devotes a singular position to maintaining the Inner European Mysteries of our pre-Christian ancestors.

In the Rooted Ways, the emphasis is upon the mated pair as they journey together through the wheel of the year. The symbolism in the cycle of life within the turning of the year reflects the journey of the soul as reincarnates. It also connects us with the presence and activity of the Divine Spirit within the seasons.

In the Rooted Ways the priestess and priest facilitate the Sabbat meal that is designed to bestow blessings and union upon those who consume it. This rite can awaken the realization within that we are the offspring of that which created the universe. It is through this that we come to know the Divine Spirit within our own being.

THE WITCH AS PRACTITIONER

In our most distant past there were people who became the first Witches. We can view them as the prototype. They developed a system through which other people eventually trained to become Witches. All of these shared a predisposition, an inner nature that carried them in the mystic Arts of Witchcraft.

There have always been people who realized they were different from most others. They saw the world differently; they felt the world differently. To them there was enchantment all around. There was something beyond and behind everyday life. This called to them to look deeper and to pay attention to what seemed to be a communication coming from somewhere seemingly hidden.

To answer that call, these individuals set out upon the practice of Witchcraft. For some people, Witchcraft is simply a personal practice void of any religious connotation. However, some practitioners work with spirits and entities that aid their Witchcraft. In this sense Witchcraft is a magical path, a personal practice of the Arts of Witchery. This form is closer to sorcery than to religious Witchcraft.

In customized Witchcraft there is typically a reliance upon the magical and ritual tools (as opposed to interaction with the gods). Special oils, herbs, and stones are used by the Witch for creating an energy of enchantment. This sense of an occult or mystical atmosphere is key to personalized Witchcraft. The idea behind working with items is that they are believed to possess a form of consciousness and a form of energy with specific abilities. From this we derive an occult table of correspondences that reveal the properties of things like crystals, herbs, animal natures, and so on.

Customized forms of Witchcraft often place an emphasis on the power of the mind. This includes establishing specific states of consciousness. These are used to empower the Witch and her or his rituals and works of magic. These altered states of consciousness can open portals within the psyche of the Witch as well as various inner dimensions of reality.

The practitioner type of Witch is independent and does not usually adhere to preestablished traditions of Witchcraft. She or he is most commonly self-educated through books, workshops, and experimental practice of the Arts. I refer to this as the self-styled Witch. The reliance here is upon one's intuition and sense of what feels right versus formal teachings and teachers.

The self-styled Witch is a trailblazer. She or he is not subject to methodology and is typically eclectic (gathering what is easily at hand from various sources). This allows for a great deal of freedom in one's personal practices. In this light, the Witch learns on her or his own, and is self-directed.

The image or depiction of the Witch has long been dictated by mainstream culture. The Witch has long been maligned, demeaned, vilified, and misrepresented. Human ignorance, superstition, and fear have created a figure that never existed. This is the Witch as only an outsider can envision.

The true Witch was, and is, a subcultural figure. The Witch does not "fit into" the larger social order, but instead makes her or his own way in the background of society. Living between and on the edge, the Witch is the untamed spirit. She or he maintains magic in a world that is burdened with the mundane.

For most people, being a Witch is not something one chooses. It is a calling, an inner nature. In the mystical sense, the soul of the Witch returns through reincarnation, experiencing many lifetimes. With each one the Witch reclaims, remembers, and continues to extend the way through the Path of the Witch. It is a sacred quest, moonlit and spirited guided. In the end, the Witch returns to the stars.

ACKNOWLEDGMENTS

What We Knew in the Night is the last book my beloved Raven Grimassi completed before his death on March 10, 2019. We literally finished the last major edits the day before his passing, and I think knowing the book was complete gave him the sense of freedom to let go and begin his journey into the next mystery of death and renewal. Raven died as he lived, conscious and aware, with his love and with the dignity of a priest of the Craft. Raven embodied an earlier generation of Witchcraft, unlike many of the things we see today, and he had a passion to not only preserve but also share what he knew. He took the Old Ways and worked them into new patterns, creating the Ash, Birch and Willow tradition. He would talk about his early training in California, and the wonderful and strange people of that era. If you were in the right place at the right time, with certain people, the door would open and teachings not found in any book would be shared with you. Raven found himself in that place many times, and by reading this book, you have found yourself in the right time and right place, with no better guide than Mr. Grimassi himself to hold open the door. I see this book as his final gift to the world, and I hope you enjoy it and put it to good use to make your life, and the world, a better place.

I would like to thank the many people who supported us during Raven's illness and the process of writing this book, including Christopher Penczak, Steve Kenson, Adam Sartwell, Theitic, Julia Radford,

Judika Illes, Deidre Catero Manea, and the initiate body of Ash, Birch and Willow. Another word of gratitude to Michael Kerber, Kathryn Sky-Peck, and Judika Illes for their heroic effort to provide a copy of the book for us to see.

Thank you for honoring and continuing the legacy of a truly profound spiritual teacher who always felt his work would be better understood in death than it was in life. While his work touched so many in his lifetime, I know the good he has done and will continue to do through his writings, teachings, students, friends, and family will continue to reach out beyond the bounds of his earthly life.

Greenwood Blessings,
Stephanie Taylor Grimassi

APPENDIX 1

THE WHITE WITCH

"O *what have you seen, my son, my son,*
That your eyes are so wild and bright?
Or what have you heard in the eerie woods,
'Twixt the gloaming and the night?"

"I have met a witch, a white white witch,
My mother, mother dear;
The glamour of earth is on my eyes,
And its music in my ear.

"For we are deafen'd by angry words,
Are blinded by tears of woe,
But she has garner'd the secret joys
That only the genii know;—

"Has learn'd from the voice of the fern-hid stream
Where all sweet thoughts abide,
And the violets have told her how they dream
In the quiet eventide;

"And they fancy, mother, the world above
Where the baby cloudlets play
Yearns down to the earth in mystic love
That shall never pass away.

"The greenwood knows it; of this sweet thought
Its murmuring tunes are made,
And the strange wild tale that is ever wrought
Through its sunshine and its shade.

"And the holy moon, as she moves along
From star to star on high,
Pours forth her light as a bridal song
And a tender lullaby.

"O mother, my mother, mother dear,
Who may the white witch be?
She has heard the things we cannot hear,
She has seen what we cannot see;

"The beauty that comes in fitful gleams,
That comes, but will not stay,
The music that steals across our dreams
From a region far away;

"What vainly I sought in pain and doubt,
The light, the form, the tone,
At a single glance she has found them out,
And made them all her own.

"And with all the music we cannot hear,
The beauty we cannot see,
O mother, mother, my mother dear,
She has wrought a charm on me."

—CHARLES GRANT, *STUDIES IN VERSE*

APPENDIX 2

INCANTATION

Lovely spirit, who dost dwell

In the bowers invisible,

By undying Hermes reared;

By Stagyric sage revered;

Where the silver fountains wander;

Where the golden streams meander;

Where the dragon vigil keeps

Over mighty treasure heaps;

Where the mystery is known,

Of the wonder working Stone;

Where the quintessence is gained,

And immortal life attained—

Spirit by this spell of power,

I call thee from thy viewless bower.

. . .

The charm is wrought—the word is spoken,

And the sealed vial broken!

Element with element

Is incorporate and blent;

Fire with water—air with earth,

As before creation's birth;

Matter gross is purified,

Matter humid rarefied;

Matter volatile is fixed,

The spirit with the clay commixed.

Laton is by azoth purged,

And the argent-vif disgorged;

And the black crow's head is ground,

And the magistery found;

And with broad empurpled wing

Springs to light the blood-red king,

By this fiery assation—

By this wondrous permutation

Spirit, from thy burning sphere

Float to earth—appear—appear!

—WILLIAM HARRISON AINSWORTH,
BALLADS: ROMANTIC, FANTASTICAL AND HUMOROUS

APPENDIX 3

THE NAMELESS WITCH

On the smouldering fire is thrown

Tooth of fox and weasel bone.

Eye of cat, and skull of rat,

And the hooked wing of bat,

Mandrake root and murderer's gore,

Henbane, hemlock, hellebore,

Stibium, storax, bdellium, borax,

Ink of cuttle-fish and feather

Of the screech-owl, smoke together,

II.

On the ground is a circle traced;

On that circle a seal is placed;

On that seal is a symbol graven;

On that symbol an orb of heaven;

By that orb is a figure shown;

By that figure a name is known:

Wandering witch it is thine own!—

But thy name must not be named,

Nor to mortal ears proclaimed.

Shut are the leaves of the Grimoire dread;

The spell is muttered—the word is said,

And that word, in a whisper drowned,

Shall to thee like a whirlwind sound.

Swift through the shivering air it flies—

Swiftly it traverses earth and skies;

Wherever thou art—above—below—

Thither that terrible word shall go.

Art thou on the waste alone,

To the white moon making moan?

Art thou, human eye eschewing,

In some cavern philters brewing?

By familiar swart attended—

By a triple charm defended—

Gatherest thou the grass that waves

O'er dank pestilential graves?—

Or on broom or goat astride,

To thy Sabbath dost thou ride?

Or with sooty imp doth match thee?

From his arms my spell shall snatch thee.

Shall it seek thee—and find thee,

And with a chain bind thee;

And through the air whirl thee,

And at my feet hurl thee!

By the word thou dreadst to hear!

Nameless witch!—appear—appear!

—WILLIAM HARRISON AINSWORTH,
BALLADS: ROMANTIC, FANTASTICAL AND HUMOROUS

WORKS CITED

Ainsworth, William Harrison. *Ballads: Romantic, Fantastical and Humorous*. London: G. Routledge & Co., 1855.

Bailey, Cyril. *Phases in the Religion of Ancient Rome*. London: Oxford University Press, 1932.

Benko, Stephen. *The Virgin Goddess: Studies in the Pagan and Christian Roots of Mariology*. Leiden, Netherlands: Brill, 2003.

Clark, H. F. "The Mandrake Fiend," *Folklore* 73, no. 4 (Winter 1962): 257–269.

Draper, John C. "Alchemy and Chemistry." In *The American Chemist* V, no. 1. July 1874, 2. *www.google.com*.

Dumézil, Georges. *Archaic Roman Religion*, vol. 1. Trans. Philip Krapp. Baltimore, MD: Johns Hopkins University Press, 1996.

Eliade, Mircea. *Patterns in Comparative Religion*. Trans. Rosemary Sheed. Lincoln: University of Nebraska Press, 1996.

Favazza, Armando R. *Bodies Under Siege: Self-Mutilation and Body Modification in Culture and Psychiatry*. Baltimore, MD: Johns Hopkins University Press, 1996.

Ferguson, Ian. *The Philosophy of Witchcraft*. London: G. G. Harrap, 1924.

Gordon, Richard. "Imagining Greek and Roman Magic," in *Witchcraft and Magic in Europe, Volume 2: Ancient Greece and Rome*. Ed. Bengt Ankarloo and Stuart Clark. Philadelphia: University of Pennsylvania Press, 1999.

Grandy, Liam. "Livy's Witch-hunts: A Study of Investigations into Veneficium Found in Livy." Master's thesis, Victoria University of Wellington, 2018. *https://researcharchive.vuw.ac.nz*.

Grant, Charles. *Studies in Verse*. London: John Pearson York Street Covent Garden, 1875.

Gray, William G. *Western Inner Workings*. York Beach, ME: Red Wheel Weiser, 1983.

Grenier, Albert. *The Roman Spirit in Religion, Thought, and Art*. New York: Alfred A. Knopf, 1926.

Grimassi, Raven. *Hereditary Witchcraft: Secrets of the Old Religion*. St. Paul, MN: Llewellyn, 1999.

Grimassi, Raven. "The Roots of Italian Witchcraft." Stregheria. *www.stregheria.com*.

Guazzo, Francesco Maria. *Compendium Maleficarum*. Trans. E. A. Ashwin. Mineola, NY: Dover Publications, 1988.

Horace. *Epodes*. Ed. David Mankin. New York: Cambridge University Press, 1995.

Huson, Paul. *Mastering Witchcraft: A Practical Guide for Witches, Warlocks, and Covens*. New York: G. P. Putnam's Sons, 1970.

Leland, Charles Godfrey. *Aradia: Or the Gospel of the Witches.* London: David Nutt, 1899.

Leland, Charles G. *Aradia: Or the Gospel of the Witches.* Trans. Mario Pazzaglini and Dina Pazzaglini. Blaine, WA: Phoenix Publishing, 1999.

Lévi, Eliphas. *The Great Secret or Occultism Unveiled.* York Beach, ME: Samuel Weiser, 1975.

Lucan. *Civil War.* Trans. Susan H. Braund. New York: Oxford University Press, 2008.

Macleod, Fiona. *Where the Forest Murmurs: Nature Essays.* London: Country Life and George Newnes, 1906.

Martin, Ruth. *Witchcraft and the Inquisition in Venice, 1550–1650.* New York: Basil Blackwell, 1989.

Michelet, Jules. *La Sorcière: The Witch of the Middle Ages,* Trans. L. J. Trotter. London: Simpkin, Marshall, and Co., 1863.

Neumann, Erich. *The Great Mother: An Analysis of the Archetype.* Trans. Ralph Manheim. Princeton, NJ: Princeton University Press, 2015.

Ogden, Daniel. *Magic, Witchcraft, and Ghosts in the Greek and Roman Worlds: A Sourcebook.* New York: Oxford University Press, 2002.

Ovid. *Metamorphoses.* Trans. David Raeburn. New York: Penguin Books, 2004.

Rose, Elliot. *A Razor for a Goat: Problems in the History of Witchcraft and Diabolism.* Toronto, ON: University of Toronto Press, 1989.

Russell, Jeffrey Burton. *A History of Witchcraft: Sorcerers, Heretics, and Pagans.* London: Thames and Hudson, 1980.

Russell, Jeffrey Burton. *Witchcraft in the Middles Ages*. Ithaca, New York: Cornell University Press, 1984.

Sharp, William. *A Memoir: Compiled by His Wife, Elizabeth A. Sharp*. New York: Duffield & Company, 1910.

Stevens, Walter. *Demon Lovers: Witchcraft, Sex, and the Crisis of Belief*. Chicago: University of Chicago Press, 2002.

Summers, Montague. *History of Witchcraft and Demonology*. Whitefish, MT: Kessinger, 2003.

Tartarotti, Girolamo. *Apologia Del Congresso Notturno Delle Lammi*. Ulan Press, 2012.

Valiente, Doreen. *Witchcraft for Tomorrow*. Blaine, WA: Phoenix Publishing, 1987.

Virgil. *The Aeneid*. Trans. John Dryden. London: George Routledge and Sons, 1887.

ABOUT THE AUTHOR

Raven Grimassi (1951-2019) is the award-winning author of over twenty books, as well as two oracle decks. He appears in the DVD *Ever Ancient, Ever New: Witchcraft by the Hearthside.* A leading authority on witchcraft, the occult, and spiritual development and a practitioner with over forty-five years of experience in esoteric traditions, Raven traveled widely to teach at magical gatherings and festivals and dedicated his life to researching, preserving, and writing about ancient pre-Christian European ways. A recognized expert on Italian witchcraft and the works of folklorist Charles Godfrey Leland, Raven was a practitioner with over forty-five years of experience in esoteric traditions.

Together with his wife Stephanie Taylor, Raven cofounded the Ash, Birch and Willow tradition of witchery and shared this work using home study courses through the House of Grimassi. Today Ash, Birch and Willow is a thriving tradition with initiates across the world. Raven and Stephanie hosted an online radio show, *Seasons of the Witch,* archived on BlogTalkRadio. Their online retail store, Raven's Loft *(ravensloft.biz),* has been dedicated to providing items for spiritual and magical practice for over nineteen years. Learn more about his legacy online at *HouseofGrimassi.com.*

TO OUR READERS

Weiser Books, an imprint of Red Wheel/Weiser, publishes books across the entire spectrum of occult, esoteric, speculative, and New Age subjects. Our mission is to publish quality books that will make a difference in people's lives without advocating any one particular path or field of study. We value the integrity, originality, and depth of knowledge of our authors.

Our readers are our most important resource, and we appreciate your input, suggestions, and ideas about what you would like to see published.

Visit our website at *www.redwheelweiser.com* to learn about our upcoming books and free downloads, and be sure to go to *www.redwheelweiser.com/newsletter* to sign up for newsletters and exclusive offers.

You can also contact us at *info@rwwbooks.com* or at

Red Wheel/Weiser, LLC
65 Parker Street, Suite 7
Newburyport, MA 01950